EMPLOYING STAFF

As employers, general practitioners have numerous legal duties that must not be neglected. Employment law is complex and constantly changing, but if you fail to keep up with it you could find yourself paying out large sums in compensation. The third edition of *Employing Staff* provides a brief guide to the basic principles and an up to date account of the latest developments as they affect small businesses. Written specially for GPs, it will also be useful to other professionals — for example, dentists and opticians.

EMPLOYING STAFF

NORMAN ELLIS MA PHD
Under secretary British Medical Association

THIRD EDITION

Articles from the *British Medical Journal*

Published by the British Medical Association
Tavistock Square,
London WCIH 9JR

.

First Edition 1984
Reprinted 1986
Second Edition 1987
Third Edition 1989

ISBN 0 7279 0270 9

Filmset and printed in Great Britain by
Latimer Trend & Company Ltd, Plymouth

Contents

Preface

In the past 20 years no fewer than 14 Acts of Parliament have been passed on employment rights, and most of these are relevant to general practitioners. More than two dozen new rights have been created for employees, and a general practitioner breaches them at his peril. We all know that "ignorance is no defence," and a general practitioner who is found at fault by an industrial tribunal may find himself paying out a five figure sum. He or she cannot be expected to become an expert on this complex matter, but somebody in each practice does need to know the guiding principles.

Those principles are brought together and laid out clearly for the first time in this important, thoroughly reliable, and yet readable book. Indeed, this is the first time that such a book has been written for small businesses, and, although written very much with the general practitioner in mind, the butcher, the baker, the candlestick maker (and certainly the dentist and the optician) will all find the book useful. It is a publisher's cliché to describe a book as indispensable, and probably no single book of clinical medicine could be so described. But I suspect that any general practitioner who has to pay out £5000 for unknowingly breaching an employee's right may be tempted to agree that for the next few years at least this book is genuinely essential.

The fact that several thousand general practitioners have bought previous editions speaks for itself.

STEPHEN LOCK
Editor
British Medical Journal
November 1984

Introduction to the Third Edition

This book brings together a series of articles on employment law and management which have been written for general practitioners. It deals with those problems that are most likely to occur in general practice. It is essential reading because as an employer you have a wide range of legal duties that you should not forget or neglect. Much of this law is complex, and because existing books and articles on this subject are written for the large corporation or company it has been necessary to provide a practical and simplified account that is accessible to the small employer.

This book is tailor made for general practitioners, most of whom employ no more than a handful of staff. Indeed, there are many other employers, particularly the professions, such as dentists, who will also find it useful. Members of the British Medical Association should contact their regional office if they require further advice and assistance.

Employment law is continually changing. Many important changes have been introduced since the first edition of this book was published in December 1984. The qualifying period for unfair dismissal has been extended to two years for all employees, regardless of the size of the employer's undertaking. Another important change has been the extension from 6 April 1986 of the period for which employers are responsible for paying statutory sick pay from 8 to 28 weeks. Statutory maternity pay was introduced on 6 April 1987.

A new Employment Bill is progressing through parliament. When enacted it is likely to exempt small businesses with fewer than 20 employees from the requirement to give employees—within 13 weeks of starting work—a note of the disciplinary procedures in the written statement of the main terms and conditions of employment. But it is still a good idea to provide the note so people know where they stand, especially as the remainder of the written statement still has to be provided by all employers. The bill will also increase from six months to two years the qualifying period for an employee to be entitled to obtain a written statement of the reasons for dismissal. Industrial tribunals may be able to require a prehearing deposit of up to £150 to deter vexatious claims. Finally, employers with fewer than 10 employees will no longer be able to claim the redundancy rebate.

This book can provide only a general guide to the provisions of existing legislation. It does not offer a definitive statement of the law.

Recruiting ancillary staff

Good recruitment and selection procedures can improve the running of your practice—for example, by reducing staff turnover. If you choose the right staff they are likely to stay with you and give good and loyal service. If you pick the wrong people they will leave voluntarily when they find more suitable employment, leave involuntarily when you decide they are not suited to the job, or you may even put up with unsatisfactory or indifferent standards of work.

Unlike large organisations the general practitioner cannot be expected to devote sizable resources to recruiting and training new staff. But the general practitioner experiences more acute difficulties than the large organisation if the staff he recruits prove to be unsatisfactory. Strong personal ties can develop among a small group of staff and any disciplinary action (which can ultimately lead to a dismissal) is often more difficult to take. It is only too common to find a doctor tolerating a poor level of performance from his staff simply because he cannot face the unpleasant and difficult task of correcting the problem.

Although the time spent on recruiting and training new staff may seem costly, it is often less costly in the long run than the resources that may be wasted when staff prove to be ill suited to their work. To neglect these matters almost always stores up trouble for the future.

Too often when a general practitioner is faced with staffing difficulties (which may even involve a threat of legal action) the roots of these lie in his failure to recruit the right staff in the first instance and to provide them with the training they require. These shortcomings may be compounded by an innate reluctance to manage. Early difficulties are left uncorrected, and unsatisfactory

1

performance and working habits are allowed to persist and are thus tolerated by all concerned. The general practitioner's failure to act in these circumstances is often interpreted (quite understandably) as evidence of his tolerance of indifferent standards of performance and unsatisfactory working practices.

When a vacancy occurs

When you have a vacancy it is essential to consider whether the vacancy really needs to be filled, and, if so, whether the content of the job has changed. (Have there been any changes in work pattern, technology—for example, computerisation—or organisation since it was last filled?) You should also consider whether there are likely to be future changes in the job which require additional or different skills. A good way of assuring yourself that the job has been thoroughly reviewed is to prepare a "job description."

It may seem pedantic to write a detailed description of the job. Is it not sufficient simply to give the job an accurate title? Unfortunately, there is no easy way of avoiding the task of preparing an adequate job description if you wish to put relations with your staff on a sound workable basis.

The job description should describe the tasks and responsibilities of the job:

(a) Main purpose of job: try to summarise this as briefly as possible. (If you cannot identify a main purpose the job may need to be reviewed.)

(b) Main tasks of the job: try to use active verbs, such as "filing," "answering," and "helping" rather than less precise terms such as "deals with," "in charge of."

(c) Scope of the job: although the "main tasks" may describe what has to be done, they may not always indicate the job's scope or importance. Under this heading you may need to emphasise the degree of accuracy or precision required and the number of people supervised.

The length and detail of your job description will vary according to the job. But it is preferable to aim at providing a clear and simple description. (See appendix for a specimen job description: this draws heavily on an original draft prepared by the Association of Medical Secretaries, Practice Administrators and Receptionists.)

The job description is important because it tells you what kind of person you need for the job. It may be used to build a profile of the type of person you would like to fill the post.

Profile of the person you need

The profile is prepared by devising a list of headings under which you can classify the attributes of the ideal candidate for your vacancy. You may prefer to draft your own headings; those in the table merely illustrate how this might be done.

Specimen profile of the person to be employed as a receptionist

Necessary	Desirable
Impact on other people	
Acceptable bearing and speech	Pleasant manner, bearing, and speech
Qualifications and experience	
Ability to type, to operate PABX telephone equipment, to carry out receptionist and general office work	RSA II typing; previous experience of receptionist work
Innate abilities	
Ready grasp of a point	Can assess priorities and make decisions quickly
Motivation	
Personal identification with the work of the practice. Interest in maintaining good relations with patients, and the efficient running of the practice	Other commitments—for example, family and domestic—are such that they would not be a prior commitment. Able to work flexibly in an emergency and to do overtime during holiday absences and (at short notice) sickness absences of other staff
Adjustment	
Steady, self reliant, good at maintaining a pleasant and reassuring relationship with patients and friendly relationship with colleagues at all levels	Able to cope with stress and pressure from both patient and doctors
Health record	
Good. In particular, there should be no previous record of illness that might lead to an abuse of drugs	

(1) Impact on other people: physical appearance, speech, and manner.

(2) Qualifications and experience: education, qualifications, previous work experience. Simple and obvious matters to be considered might include clarity of handwriting, typing, and audio or shorthand skills.

(3) Ability to learn: speed of comprehension; ability to acquire new skills, etc.

(4) Commitment: what goals does the candidate set for himself or herself? Does he or she pursue these with consistency and determination? How successful has he or she been in achieving them? In particular you should know whether the candidate is seeking work to widen his or her interests—for example, to get out of the house, to have a break from family commitments. Family commitments, if pressing or extensive, can understandably soon take priority over work. Sudden absences for these reasons can cause chaos among a small staff.

(5) Personality: emotional stability; capacity to work under pressure and to deal with stress; is he or she likely to get on with your other staff, the doctors, and the patients? Another factor which employers in the health sector need to be aware of is its tendency to attract applicants who have a preoccupation with illness (particularly their own ailments).

(6) Health record: in general you should be looking for a good health record. A small practice inevitably finds it more difficult to cope with frequent or long absences. (In particular you will need to be cautious about any previous psychiatric illness that might lead to drug abuse.)

The characteristics identified as necessary from an analysis of your job description should then be entered against the appropriate heading. It is often helpful to enter two levels, indicating what you would be looking for in the ideal candidate, and what you regard as a minimum acceptable level to do the job satisfactorily. In addition, you should list any personal characteristics or circumstances which would definitely be unacceptable; for example, you would not wish to employ as your receptionist anyone who had an abrasive manner.

An example of a completed profile based on the specimen job description is provided below. How much detail is included in the personnel profile will depend on the job, but not always on the level of the post; for example, a junior post can have important requirements under the heading "impact on other people."

If the personnel profile is used as a basis for your interviews it will remind you to be both realistic and systematic. But it must be remembered that there is nothing precise or scientific about a selection procedure. By being systematic you will help to reduce the margin of error. Ultimately you must decide which of the candidates is best suited to fill the job. If after completing the interviews you think that no candidate is suitable, do not hesitate to defer an appointment.

Finding suitable applicants

Having written the job description and the personnel profile, you now need to consider the best way of reaching the "target group" of potential candidates. One method that is often used by general practitioners is by word of mouth, sometimes from introductions made by other staff or even patients. This has obvious attractions; it costs nothing and it helps you to recruit those people from the immediate locality who may have ties of friendship or family with your present staff and the practice. But it may have the disadvantage of perpetuating the existing composition of your staff and it might even lead to allegations of unlawful discrimination. There is also the hidden danger of relaxing your critical faculties and subsequently departing from your carefully prepared personnel profile. It is far too easy to be drawn into appointing someone about whom you feel reassured simply because they have been personally recommended to you, without having evaluated him or her against your criteria of selection. If this happens and your new member of staff is subsequently found to be unsatisfactory, the already testing business of dismissal is compounded by the family and personal ties with your other staff.

Many general practitioners have to recruit staff from the area in which their surgeries are located. Sometimes they recruit staff from among their patients. The problems of confidentiality are obvious enough, and at times it may be friends and relatives who pose the greatest potential threat to confidentiality. It is sufficient to emphasise this problem and you should ensure that all staff, particularly new members of staff, are aware of the importance of maintaining absolute confidentiality and that any breach of confidentiality will be treated as a serious disciplinary matter.

Local schools, colleges, and career services can provide many candidates who may be suited for your post; but if you recruit from these sources you will need to pay extra attention to your arrangements for training new staff. The local newspaper is often the most consistently reliable method of finding candidates, though it can be costly.

Application forms

You may choose between using a standard application form, asking for letters of application, or simply taking down information over the phone or at the interview. The advantage of using an application form is that it is easier to compare like with like, thus helping with the initial sifting of candidates. You, not the candidates, determine what information is included and the form may be a basis for the interviewer. The standard of completion may be a guide to the candidate's suitability, particularly if clerical skills are important to the job. But application forms do lengthen the selection process and add to your clerical and administrative costs.

Selecting the best candidate

For most vacancies you may want to receive written applications in advance of the interviews and to arrange a simple practical test. (It is common practice to test typing and shorthand skills.)

Your partners and you will need to decide who should be on the interviewing panel. If you have a practice administrator or manager you may wish him or her to participate in the selection of a receptionist. The extent to which the practice manager or administrator will participate in the selection will depend on the particular circumstances of your practice. In some practices the practice manager may carry out a preliminary sift of applications by a first interview, reducing a large number of candidates to a final shortlist. These shortlisted candidates are then asked back for a second interview with some of the partners. At the very least you should allow your practice administrator to express a view before a final decision is made. The likelihood of the new employee settling successfully into your practice depends to a great extent on the person who supervises the work and is responsible for seeing that the new recruit is properly trained and made to feel welcome. If your practice administrator has helped in the selection of the new employee he or she will naturally feel more committed to the employee. Similarly, it is often advisable for the candidate to meet the rest of the staff before a decision is made.

References can be helpful but these should be used with care. They are often most useful for checking factual information such as details of previous jobs (length of service, absenteeism, time keeping, etc). It is particularly important to check on the applicant's previous record of absenteeism and sickness. If you want an opinion on suitability for a specific job, a brief outline of the duties should be sent to the referee and a subsequent telephone conversation may be helpful.

The interview

Although most jobs are still filled by interview, doubts have been expressed about this method of selection. Despite its limitations, it is widely used and general practitioners will undoubtedly wish to use it to select their staff.

For your interviews to be effective you need to do some preparation, and they will need to be conducted in an orderly and thorough manner. The interview need not be an overformal or elaborate exercise.

Three other points need to be remembered at the outset. Firstly, you should consider preparing a check list of the points to be raised. Secondly, you may inadvertently enter into contractual obligations (albeit verbal) either in reply to an unexpected question or merely in your attempts to reassure the candidate. Do leave an escape route by emphasising that the employment contract will be in writing and that it will cover all relevant matters. Thirdly, throughout the interviews you should ensure that none of your questions or answers can be interpreted as discriminatory on grounds of race, colour, nationality (including citizenship), or ethnic or national origins. It is also unlawful for employers to discriminate on grounds of sex or against married persons. Discrimination is prohibited in recruitment and in relation to existing employees. Employers with fewer than six employees are no longer excluded under the Sex Discrimination Act.

Your preparation should include the following:

(1) Compare the personnel profile with what you already know about the candidate. Are there any areas of experience or qualifications, for instance, which will need to be explored or clarified? For

7

example, you may decide to test typing, shorthand, and audio skills, and also assess the clarity of handwriting.

(2) Plan your questions. These should probe the candidate's knowledge, ability, and attitudes. Some questions should be aimed at a more general assessment of the candidate. In this area you may wish to explore in some detail the candidate's domestic and family commitments—for example, children, elderly relatives, and even pets. How extensive are these? Are they likely to take priority over his or her work, and how often is this likely to occur? The health record will need to be discussed and you may wish to seek the candidate's agreement to approach his or her general practitioner. Ease of travel to work can be important, together with flexibility in approach to working hours. Few practices can work with a rigid attitude to stopping at a fixed time when the bell goes. Finally, the candidate's motives for changing jobs or seeking employment, or both, are relevant.

(3) If there is more than one interviewer allocate the subjects to be covered.

(4) Provide an opportunity for the candidate to ask questions and anticipate the information needed to answer the most likely ones.

(5) Be organised, allow enough time, avoid interruptions, and have someone available to show candidates to the cloakroom, waiting room, etc.

Poor interviews are usually caused by the interviewer being unprepared and unaware of how demanding interviewing can be. In these circumstances the interviewer may talk more than the interviewee and ask leading questions to which the answers are far too obvious. In addition, important aspects of the candidate's previous experience, qualifications, views, and attitudes may be left unexplored, so that a proper comparison of candidates cannot be made.

It is useful to have shown the candidate the job description beforehand and to have a copy of your contract of employment to hand during the interview. Do ask the candidate if he or she has any questions about the job description. Do not hesitate to mention any demanding and important aspects of the job. It is far better for the candidate to learn at this stage than later about any aspect of the job he or she may not like. It is also advisable to show the candidates around the surgery, letting them see what work has to be done, before asking them to commit themselves to the job.

After the interview

After each interview is completed write up notes on your impressions, recording any points strongly for or against the candidate. This will help you to make your final decision, particularly if others participate in the discussion. These notes will also help you to monitor the effectiveness and fairness of your procedures. Your reasons for appointing or not appointing a particular candidate may be important in case you are challenged—for example, under the sex discrimination or race relations legislation. (It may be worth retaining your notes to refer to if a further vacancy occurs.)

When you have taken your decision inform all the applicants of the outcome. (It cannot be emphasised too often that if you have doubt about the suitability of your preferred candidates do not hesitate to defer the appointment and seek new candidates.) Your letter offering the job should say the date on which employment starts and cover the main headings of the contract. It should also refer to the employment contract which will be issued after the employee has started work.

Benefits of good recruitment procedures

Good recruitment and selection procedures are likely to provide you with the right people for your jobs. Your practice administrator or manager should participate in the recruitment. He or she will have to work with the person who is selected and probably play a major part in the training of the new member of staff.

Before you interview any candidates it is essential to analyse the job to be filled and to consider what type of person would be capable of filling it. By completing these tasks beforehand you can be more assured of fitting the right person into the right job.

Finally, having put this effort into the recruitment and selection of staff, do not forget or neglect to ensure that they are properly trained to do the job. Training is especially important if your new recruit is a school leaver or a person returning to work after a period away from it. (You may wish to plan for a period of overlap. If the practice is not using its full "quota" of ancillary staff a trainee could overlap with the present job occupant and the practice could receive its 70% reimbursement.)

I am grateful to Dr John Ball and Dr Ewen Bramwell for their advice. I am, of course, responsible for any omissions or errors.

Appendix

Specimen job description

Job title: receptionist

Main purpose of job: to ensure
   (i) that inquiries from patients are efficiently and courteously handled
   (ii) that the filing, record keeping, and distribution of documents is undertaken efficiently and promptly
   (iii) that the surgery premises are kept tidy

Main duties:

   1 Opening the premises and checking heating and ventilation
   2 Restoring telephone services
   3 Distributing patients' records to the doctors for their surgeries and ensuring that the records or any patients without appointments are available to the doctor when the patient is seen
   4 Setting out letters, new prescriptions, and repeat prescriptions for checking by the doctor before collection
   5 Receiving and routing patients on arrival
   6 Answering general inquiries, explaining surgery procedures, making new and follow up appointments, and receiving requests for repeat prescriptions
   7 Filing and extracting records and any documents relating to these including:
   (i) filing records of new patients received from the family practitioner committee
   (ii) extracting records of withdrawals from list to send to family practitioner committee
   8 Receiving and recording requests for home visits
   9 Ensuring that an adequate supply of stationery is available in the consulting rooms and the reception area
   10 Receiving messages for nurses and health visitors
   11 Ventilating and tidying waiting room after surgery
   12 Ensuring that the reception area is left tidy and ready for use by incoming colleagues, together with information about any unresolved or urgent matters
   13 Making tea or coffee for the doctors

Looking after your new employee

If you have expended effort on recruiting good staff it would be pointless to dissipate this by failing to help them to become accustomed to your practice and to do their jobs satisfactorily. It may seem self evident that any new employee should be properly trained and introduced into the practice, but it is surprising how often employers neglect or forget this essential task. Your staff are a vital asset to your practice, and you owe it to them and to yourself to ensure that they are able to contribute to the best of their abilities. If you fail to provide adequate induction and training you may leave yourself seriously at risk if you ever need to take disciplinary action. The term "induction" may be unfamiliar to you and you may reasonably assume that it is yet another example of technical jargon intruding into the English language, but its use may be justified because it encapsulates the specific task that any employer should undertake.

Why "induction" matters

You need to help your new employee to settle into the practice as quickly as possible. This means that she should be helped to get to know her colleagues and the partners, to become familiar with the surgery premises, and to know the wider contacts that will be an important part of her job (these may be other practices, the local health authority, local hospitals, the social services department, and the family practitioner committee). Above all, she will need to be helped in getting to grips with the job. Of course, a lot of this knowledge may be "picked up" gradually without any formal induction programme. But there are good reasons for ensuring that this wide range of information is acquired in a planned and systematic way.

When someone starts a new job there is usually some anxiety about certain aspects of the job. She is faced with new colleagues, a new boss, new tasks, and a new environment. Helping your new employee to settle in is not just a matter of courtesy and consideration, it also contributes to the smooth running of your practice. Induction may be just as important in a small organisation as it is for those large organisations which run formal training courses, and properly done it need not be costly in time or resources. But if you neglect or forget it, it may be very expensive indeed.

Until your new employee has settled down she is unlikely to be fully responsive to the demands of her job. There is always an initial (and often steep) learning curve to be surmounted and until this is achieved she is unlikely to respond quickly and effectively to the demands of the new job. The time lag that occurs before a satisfactory performance is achieved is likely to be increased if there is no induction programme. Your instructions (or more likely those coming from your practice manager) may be misunderstood or forgotten, and important procedures may be neglected. Your new employee's initial enthusiasm for the job may simply wane before she begins to feel settled, and she may soon become disenchanted and even resign. If discontented your new employee is unlikely to be effective and may even cause friction in the practice. A new and inexperienced colleague may even have an unsettling influence (albeit unintended) on your existing staff, so there is a strong case for speeding up her integration into the practice. If you get your induction programme right you can avoid these problems. You will have positively helped your new recruit to settle in and to develop a loyalty and commitment to your practice. Of course, if she becomes disenchanted and leaves all the time and effort that you have spent on recruitment has been wasted.

When should induction start?

In fact "induction" actually begins when you are recruiting the new employee. Any applicant for your vacancy should learn something about general practice and how your surgery runs. She is likely to form some first impressions of prospective colleagues (see "Recruiting ancillary staff"). After she has been selected for the post it may be helpful to invite her to meet her new colleagues informally before accepting the job. In a small, tight knit unit it is crucial that staff are compatible and that conflicts of personality should not occur.

The next stage is to ensure that there is a welcome on the first day. Although your practice manager may be busy and preoccupied with the normal daily pressures of the surgery, she should make a special effort to give the newcomer her full attention. Many employers ask the recruit to come later on the first day—for example, after morning surgery has ended—so that the practice manager may then give her undivided attention.

Induction may be spread over several days, or even weeks. In a small organisation it should not take long. However short the induction programme, it should be comprehensive. Any newcomer can absorb only a limited amount of information at a time, but, on the other hand, the more established she becomes the more difficult it is to set aside time for induction. It is important to allow time for your new employee to gain confidence in her new job. There is likely to be a high and continuous pressure of work from the moment she arrives until the end of the day. It is unlikely that this pressure of work was experienced in a previous job. It may even lead to an early resignation from the job. Thus it is important to ensure that she is gradually eased into the new working pattern.

What kind of training is needed?

Although induction training is usually informal, particularly in a small organisation, it should nevertheless follow a defined plan. Ideally this "plan" should be written down (perhaps in a checklist) to ensure that you neither forget nor neglect anything. If your new recruit is a receptionist your practice manager will need to be closely concerned in preparing this plan and implementing it. Indeed, most (if not all) of the induction process may need to be undertaken by your practice manager, or another member of your staff. Not all practices have a practice manager, however. Thus one of the partners should be responsible for administration and he would normally ensure that induction is properly completed. Even where there is a practice manager it is often most helpful for one of the partners to take a personal interest in the new member of staff.

This allows working relationships with the doctors to be developed, it ensures that the methods and objectives of the practice are not diluted or misinterpreted, and it may even give the doctor greater insight into the daily running of the practice.

Normally, induction requires your new recruit to listen to other members of your staff talk about their work and how the practice runs. Your employee will also be watching the pattern of work activities and she should of course be encouraged to ask questions, however basic or simple. In addition, you may wish to use your written statement of terms and conditions of employment and the job description to help explain how the practice is organised (see "Employment law").

Who needs induction?

Anyone who is new to your practice (or even someone who is transferred from another job) needs some induction. But there are particular groups of people who may need special help and advice. It is not surprising to find that no induction is provided for an employee who is transferred from another job or promoted. Often it may not be necesary. But it is never advisable to assume that a highly competent receptionist will automatically become an effective practice manager immediately after promotion. Indeed, internal promotions in a small organisation may create special difficulties; you should not expect someone to easily assume managerial authority and responsibility over colleagues who were formerly her "equals." If the promotion is to be successful for all concerned one of the partners may need to put aside time regularly to advise and assist the newly promoted practice manager. You should not assume that someone who was recruited from a similar position in another practice will easily slot into your practice. New staff from other practices may have firmly developed preconceptions about how the job should be done, which do not fit in with your own arrangements. They may need retraining to understand and apply the methods and philosophy of your practice.

Certain other groups may need special help. School leavers or young people without any experience of employment may be excited yet nervous about their first job. Indeed, they may need to be helped in a sympathetic but firm way to understand the discipline of working life, in particular punctuality, reliability, courtesy to patients, and the need to have a positive attitude to work. Women returning to work after a long absence may also find difficulty when readjusting to working life. Special help may also be needed if you employ a disabled person or a member of a minority racial group.

Who does the induction?

Although several people may be concerned in the induction programme, it is advisable to identify one person who has overall responsibility for this task. In most practices the practice administrator will have the main responsibility (and the greatest interest) in ensuring that your new employee settles in and quickly becomes an effective member of your staff. If the newcomer is a receptionist or secretary then your practice administrator or another experienced member of your staff will be best equipped to provide much of the initial training. They will be most familiar with the newcomer's job and close at hand to advise and assist. Above all, someone must be given specific responsibility for this task; your new employee should know who to turn to when seeking guidance or reassurance.

Important task often neglected

How you approach the induction of your new employees will clearly depend on the circumstances of your practice and the resources that you can devote to it. Induction need not be an elaborate business, but it should be well thought out, planned ahead, and then undertaken with care.

The effort and care that you and your staff commit to the induction of a newcomer should result in a more effective and settled employee. Although it may be self evident that any employer would want to ensure that a new employee is quickly trained to do the job and encouraged to feel at home in the practice, this task is often neglected. It is too easy to assume that the newcomer will automatically acquire the necessary skills and knowledge for the job and there is no need to make any special arrangements for this learning process.

When induction is completed this does not mean that training has ended. You may wish to encourage your staff to attend training

15

and continuing education courses. The Association of Medical Secretaries, Practice Administrators and Receptionists and the Association of Health Centre and Practice Administrators are the qualifying bodies in this field and also the principal organisations responsible for running courses for practice staff. You may wish to ascertain when you interview prospective candidates whether they have an interest in training.

I am most grateful to Dr Ewen Bramwell and Mr Peter Syson and his colleagues of ACAS for their comments on this paper. I am, of course, responsible for any omissions or errors.

Employment law

I: Why you need to know about it

General practitioners who employ staff have certain legal responsibilities, but many of them are unaware of these. Whenever I meet a group of general practitioners I usually find that more than half of them have not provided written contracts to their staff, even though the law requires this to be done. This does not mean that no contract actually exists. A verbal (unwritten) contract exists when an offer of a job is made and accepted. And this contract can last for years on a verbal and unwritten basis, capable of being interpreted and enforced by the courts. But verbal contracts, although superficially attractive for their flexibility and apparent simplicity, may lead to serious problems if differences of opinion arise. This is why successive governments, both Conservative and Labour, have introduced legislation to promote written employment contracts.

Surprisingly, but understandably, the employment relationship is so often left undocumented. The general practitioner has little time to devote to the task of writing down the various details of a contract—for example, sick pay, holidays, pensions, and disciplinary and grievance procedures—and it often seems preferable to allow these to evolve "naturally" as the working relationship develops. A written contract is not only troublesome to prepare, but might jeopardise a happy working relationship by introducing into it excessive formality and inflexibility. Because working relations between the doctor and his staff are close, the formal written contract is seen as an intrusion, bringing the formality of the law into what are essentially personal human relations. This reason is also given to explain away forgetfulness.

But the neglect of the written contract is also surprising. Irrespective of whether it is written or not, a legal contract of employment does exist, and therefore the law already has a major part to play. The value of documentation is simply to state in writing the agreements and understandings that already define relationships between the doctor and his staff. There are many other contractual relations—for example, partnership agreements, car purchase, television rental, bank loans—which no doctor would consider entering into without proper documentation spelling out in detail the agreement with the other party. But the employment contract may entail far greater liabilities and costs than even a rental or purchase agreement if it should turn sour. Yet the rights and obligations of this contract are often left to verbal understandings and agreements, which may so easily lead to misunderstandings and disagreements.

A simple precaution

I will not attempt to describe the plethora of employment law. This would be fruitless; the general practitioner has enough to worry about without trying to become an expert on employment matters. Instead, I advise general practitioners on a course of action that is simple to follow and which should help him to avoid most pitfalls.

Firstly, I would advise any general practitioner who has not already done so to consider providing *written* contracts of employment to his ancillary staff. Of course, I would also advise the doctor to exercise great caution before rushing into the surgery with a bundle of written contracts. Such a gesture can be easily misunderstood, creating, rather than avoiding, problems.

Secondly, if care is taken in preparing the contract it will take full account of existing employment law and clarify many matters where there is uncertainty on both sides. The draft contract, which appears further on, takes full account of existing statute law. It even takes account of health and safety legislation by including a policy statement on health and safety at work. (The Health and Safety at Work Act requires every employer of five or more staff to prepare a *written* statement of his general policy, organisation, and arrangements for health and safety at work.)

Finally, the British Medical Association's regional offices can

18

provide specialist advice and help to BMA members on how to introduce written contracts among ancillary staff. This service has already been widely used by members, and many general practitioners have made use of the draft contract provided.

Why is there so much employment law?

When I discuss employment law with doctors and explain its implications for general practitioners I am often asked why there is so much employment law. My answer refers to the various influences that have contributed to its growth. (Some 16 new Acts of Parliament have been implemented since the mid-1960s, establishing over 20 new rights for the individual employee.) Successive Conservative and Labour governments have tried to influence the behaviour of unions by devising laws that would encourage them to act more reasonably and responsibly. As a quid pro quo for restrictions on certain union actions—for example, picketing, secondary boycotts, closed shop—governments have provided legal ground rules covering such matters as dismissal, union recognition, discrimination, and health and safety at work. Three important episodes illustrate the "trade off" between these two sets of objectives: *In Place of Strife* and Mrs Barbara Castle's proposals for legislation; *Fair Deal at Work* and the 1970 Conservative Government's Industrial Relations Act; and the 1974 Labour Government's Employment Protection Act.

But this plethora of legislation is not merely one side of an equation designed to contain the challenge that unions pose for governments. Governments have also believed that the more formal and equitable approach to industrial relations and personnel matters required in these enactments would quickly reduce the number of disputes by improving industrial relations. Of course, there were other influences—comparisons with established international standards, for example the Equal Pay Act and Sex Discrimination Act; the influence of legislation in other subjects such as the Race Relations Act; and the commitment of governments to a climate of increased job security—for example, the Redundancy Payments Act and Industrial Training Act—that would encourage employees to relax restrictive practices and accept changes in working practices and new technology.

The law has been designed, however, to alter the personnel

practices and policies of large organisations where unions are already well established. The special position of the small employer, whose circumstances are considerably different, has been mostly ignored by legislators, but the 1980 Employment Act has made some important concessions. Many of these ground rules—the rights of the employee and the duties of the employer— apply irrespective of the size and resources of the organisation or firm.

It should be remembered that most of this law has the support of both major political parties. Both have contributed to its growth and both now accept it as a permanent feature of the industrial relations environment. Only on a few issues such as the closed shop, picketing and strike ballots is there a main divergence of opinion between Conservative and Labour Governments. This needs to be emphasised because some people who have preferred to ignore the legislation have done so on the wholly erroneous asumption that the tide would rapidly recede after the change of government in May 1979. In fact, quite the reverse seems to have occurred: the body of employment legislation is still growing, as is evident from the 1980 Employment Act.

What importance does legislation have for the small employer?

Because governments have been heavily criticised for ignoring the problems of the small employer, some thought has now been given to the importance of the legislation. The previous government made a survey of the problems of the small employer, the results of which showed that the legislation had had a limited impact. Only one small employer in 10 had had a case of unfair dismissal brought against him in the past two years. The results also showed that small employers have very few disputes and problems. When asked, "What would you say have been the main difficulties you have faced in the past year in running your business?" employment legislation and health and safety regulations were hardly mentioned.

These findings could be said to vindicate those who have preferred to ignore the legislation and carried on regardless, believing that too much fuss has been made about the risks for the small employer and that this survey gives a realistic perspective to it. This view may be acceptable to many employers who prefer to remain ignorant of the legislation (though ignorance of the law is no defence if legal proceedings should arise), but there are good reasons for being more cautious. Firstly, the survey's evidence was gathered about five years ago, and it is reasonable to assume that the climate of industrial relations has continued to change since then; more employees are becoming aware of their employment rights, and the process of unionisation is even penetrating general practice. About eight unions actively compete for members—the Guild of Medical Secretaries, APEX, MSF, NALGO, NUPE, COHSE, MATSA (GMWU clerical and executive section), and ACTS (TGWU clerical and executive sections)*—as the effects of changes in National Health Service industrial relations spill over into this related field of employment.

I have focused on the need for a written employment contract because this offers an easy remedy for the many doctors who prefer to keep employment law at a safe and decent distance. A draft contract that should suit the circumstances of most general practitioners, with advice on how it might be introduced, are provided in this chapter.

Avoid litigation by good management

I must emphasise that the overriding aim should be to avoid litigation. When doctors ask for help with problems concerning their ancillary staff they often mistakenly look for legal solutions to problems that are caused simply by their failure to manage their staff effectively. For example, one doctor asked if the law could help him to persuade his receptionist to provide him with a cup of tea twice a day, morning and late afternoon. (At the time I met the doctor he was actually making tea twice daily for his receptionist.) This doctor had not established control as a manager 14 years earlier when he first conceded that his receptionist should no longer undertake this task as part of her job only a few days after she started work. At the time he did not like to say anything,

*APEX, Association of Professional, Executive, Clerical and Computer Staff. MSF, NALGO, National and Local Government Officers' Association. NUPE, National Union of Public Employees. COHSE, Confederation of Health Service Employees. MATSA, Managerial, Administrative, Technical and Supervisory Section (of the National Union of General and Municipal Workers—GMWU). ACTS, Association of Clerical, Technical and Supervisory Staffs (of the Transport and General Workers' Union—TGWU).

believing it would cause unpleasantness. And he hoped that the difficulty would improve. But the question of who made the tea was just the tip of an iceberg: below the surface their working relations had been unsatisfactory from the outset, and these had deteriorated further over the years. The law as such had little to offer this doctor in the way of a remedy. The problem had been allowed to drift on for far too long, and it needed more than legal action to put it right.

This example is typical of many cases where BMA advice is sought. It illustrates some of the advantages of a more formal approach to the employment relationship. It should provide a firm foundation for good working relations. The written contract should also describe the disciplinary procedure that would be invoked if performance in the job was unsatisfactory.

The prescription of a more formal approach to such matters, relying on properly agreed and documented contracts, might be regarded as overreacting to something of minor importance. But this is simply not so. Poor relations between the doctor and his receptionist may seriously undermine his efficiency as a practitioner, and where there is only a small number of staff the problems are often more difficult to handle.

In my experience many of the problems of general practitioners are caused by poor selection procedures when staff are first appointed, inadequate supervision, and a reluctance to act decisively when staff are found to be unsatisfactory. Of course, for the general practitioner who employs only a few staff it is pointless to recommend formal procedures drawn from the practices of large organisations for the recruitment, appointment, and discipline of staff. The best advice that can be offered is that basic commonsense principles should be applied to these matters. The general practitioner should take great care to recruit the right staff, they should serve a probationary period (say, nine months) with effective procedures for assessing their performance, and the general practitioner should not hesitate to take firm action if their performance fails to meet the standard required.

II: Importance of the employment contract

A contract of employment exists as soon as an employee proves his acceptance of an employer's terms and conditions of employment by starting work, and both employer and employee are bound by the terms offered and agreed. Often the initial agreement is verbal and not written down. But within 13 weeks of an employee starting work the employer must give him a written statement about the main terms of employment with an additional note on disciplinary and grievance procedures. (This requirement does not cover employees who normally work fewer than 16 hours, unless they have worked for eight or more hours a week for five years.) I recommend that contracts should be provided for all staff, whether part time or full time.

Irrespective of what the minimal legal requirement may be, there is every reason to treat the employment contract as an important legal transaction between the two parties and to document it properly. If this is done the documentation should at least avoid those disputes of interpretation which are simply "your word against mine". The employer is legally obliged to provide an employee within 13 weeks of starting work a written statement which either contains (or refers to another document containing) the following particulars:

(1) Name of the parties
(2) Date employment began and statement about continuity
(3) Job title
(4) Pay
(5) Hours
(6) Holiday and holiday pay provisions
(7) Sick pay
(8) Pension
(9) Notice
(10) Grievance, disciplinary, and appeals procedures. (This specific requirement will be modified for employers with fewer than 20 staff when the new Employment Bill is enacted in 1989.)

It thus seems only sensible to take the exercise a stage further by preparing and issuing a comprehensive contract of employment that includes these.

Once you get the contract of employment right then you have gone a long way towards ensuring that unforeseen disputes do not arise from current employment legislation. This is because the task of preparing and agreeing the contract has made sure that you are familiar with current employment law and have not unknowingly acted contrary to it at the outset. In addition, if any dispute should arise and you find yourself having to defend your personnel practices and policies, your position will be greatly strengthened if it can be shown that you acted in good faith and had taken reasonable steps to act in accordance with the law.

Rights of the employee

In this section I summarise the main employment rights. It is not a comprehensive list; a few selected employment rights which have only limited relevance to the general practitioner have been omitted—for example, those concerned with suspension on medical grounds, the right to receive guaranteed pay, the insolvency of an employer, and the rehabilitation of offenders.

(i) Contract of employment

(a) After four weeks' employment the employee is given the right to a certain minimum period of notice, dependent on length of service, and will usually be entitled to pay during notice. Similarly, after four weeks' employment the employee is required to give a minimum notice of one week.

(b) Employers must provide employees with a written statement of the main terms and conditions of their employment.

(ii) Itemised pay statement

An employer must provide each employee with an itemised pay statement, which shows gross pay and take home pay, and the amounts and reasons for all variable deductions. The statement must show the amount and reason for each fixed deduction, or alternatively the total amount of all fixed deductions with the amounts and reasons given in a separate annual statement.

(iii) Trade union membership and activities

An employer may not lawfully take any action against an employee for being a member of, or for taking part at an appropriate time in the activities of, an independent trade union. An employer may also not take any action against an employee to compel him to join a non-independent trade union, or to compel him to join an independent trade union in a closed shop if he genuinely objects to membership on grounds of conscience or other deeply held personal convictions.

(iv) Time off work

(a) *Time off for trade union duties and activities*

An employee who is an official of an independent trade union, which is recognised by the employer, must be allowed reasonable time off with pay to carry out trade union duties if these are concerned with industrial relations between the employer and his employees. An employee who is a member of an independent trade union that is recognised by the employer is entitled to reasonable time off for certain trade union activities. The employer is not obliged to pay the employee for time off for trade union activities.

(b) *Time off for public duties*

An employer is also required, under certain circumstances, to permit any employee who holds certain public positions reasonable time off to perform these duties. This covers such offices as Justice of the Peace, members of a local authority, members of any statutory tribunal, and members of certain health, education, water, and river authorities. The employer is not obliged to pay the employee for the time off he takes for public duties.

(c) *Redundancy and time off to look for work*

An employee who is being made redundant, and who has been continuously employed by his employer for at least two years, is entitled to take reasonable time off with pay to look for another job or to make arrangements for training for future employment.

(d) *Time off for antenatal care*

Any employee who is pregnant may not be unreasonably refused time off with pay to attend appointments for antenatal care. Other than in the case of the first appointment during the pregnancy, an employer is entitled to see a certificate from a registered medical practitioner, midwife, or health visitor stating that the employee is pregnant, and to see evidence of the appointments.

(v) Rights of the expectant mother

(a) *The right to return to a job*

A woman who is expecting a baby, and who has worked for her

employer continuously for at least two years has the right not to be dismissed because of pregnancy, unless her condition makes it impossible for her to do her job adequately or her continued employment would be against the law. (In these circumstances she must be offered a suitable alternative job if one is available.)

(b) *The rights to receive statutory maternity pay and to return to work*

To have the right to statutory maternity pay (SMP) an employee must have at least 26 weeks' recent continuous employment up and into the fifteenth week before the expected week of confinement, normal weekly earnings of not less than the National Insurance (NI) lower limit, and have given 21 days' prior notice of intended absence and provided evidence of confinement. Employees paying reduced rate NI contributions, part timers and "casual" or temporary staff are also entitled to SMP if they satisfy these conditions. SMP is payable once an employee has stopped work if she satisfies the above conditions. It is paid for 18 weeks from any date between the eleventh and sixth week before the expected date of confinement.

An employee has the right to return to her former job (or suitable alternative work) at any time before the end of 29 weeks beginning with the week in which her child is born if she satisfies the following conditions. She must have been continuously employed for at least two years immediately before the beginning of the eleventh week before the expected date of confinement if she normally works for 16 or more hours per week, or for five years if she works for eight to 16 hours. She must continue to be employed (whether or not she is actually attending work) until immediately before the beginning of the eleventh week before the expected week of confinement. She must normally tell the employer, in writing, at least 21 days before her maternity absence, that she intends to return to work. She must also give written notice of her return at least 21 days before her return.

She may not have the right to return if (1) the employer has five or fewer employees and can show that it is not reasonably practicable for her to be taken back or (2) her former job is no longer there because of redundancy and there is no suitable alternative.

Furthermore the employer may request (not earlier than 49 days after the notified confinement week/date) written confirmation of her intention to return. This request should be in writing and warn that failure to write back within 14 days of receipt will debar the right to return. The right to return may be exercised at any time up to 29 weeks beginning with the week in which the child was born. The date of return may be extended beyond this in certain specified instances.

Nevertheless the right to return shall not apply where the total number of employees did not exceed five (at the time immediately before the maternity absence began) *and* it was not reasonably practicable for the employer to permit her to return.

Finally, any employer who takes on a temporary replacement for an employee who has stopped work to have a baby should advise the replacement (in writing, at the time of engagement) that the employment will be terminated when the original employee returns.

(vi) Unfair dismissal

Employees have the right not to be unfairly dismissed, and employees who think they have been unfairly dismissed may seek a remedy by complaining to an industrial tribunal.

Unfair dismissal has worried many general practitioners. It is important and is discussed in detail separately.

(vii) Redundancy pay

Employers are required to make a lump sum compensation payment called a "redundancy payment", to certain employees dismissed because of redundancy with at least two years' continuous service. The amount is related to the employee's age, length of service with the employer, and weekly pay.

(viii) Sex and race discrimination

It is unlawful for any employer to discriminate on grounds of sex or against married persons. It is also unlawful to discriminate on racial grounds—that is, on the grounds of race, colour, nationality (including citizenship), or ethnic or national origins. Discrimination is prohibited by employers in recruitment and in relation to existing employees—for example, in training and promotion. The same principle also applies to partnerships, irrespective of size.

(ix) Equal pay

Employers are required to afford equal treatment to men and women who are employed on "like work", work rated as equivalent and work of equal value. Equal pay is, therefore, not restricted to remuneration alone, but includes all terms of a contract of employment other than those relating to death or retirement benefits.

Remedies available to employees

The remedy for an alleged breach of contract lies at present with the civil courts. The remedies where written statements of the terms and conditions of employment are concerned lie with industrial tribunals. The tribunal has power only to determine what particulars the written statement shall include; it does not have the power to arbitrate where any of the particulars is in dispute. Such cases are dealt with by the civil courts. The various remedies for unfair dismissal have been explained above.

Remedies under all the other provisions outlined above lie with industrial tribunals, and in some cases where an employer is found not to have complied with one or more of the provisions the tribunal may make an award of compensation to be paid by the employer to the employee.

How to introduce a written contract

Once a doctor has decided to introduce written contracts among his staff there is a risk that he may act hastily and cause unnecessary anxiety. It is important not to upset staff who have served the practice loyally over many years by suddenly asking them to sign and exchange written contracts. A useful approach might be to treat the whole exercise as something which was being "imposed" on the practice from outside. The next stage, then requires discussing in detail what the written contract might contain, bearing in mind the draft document that is discussed next. It is possible that some matters may be unclear, and it may be necessary to clarify the details of certain terms and conditions of service—for example, sick leave and holiday provisions. What often emerges during this exercise is that there are inexplicable variations between the terms and conditions of different staff, which have simply evolved on an ad hoc basis. In the next chapter I will explain how you can best change the terms and conditions of an existing contract.

III: The contract

This is a draft contract of employment for the general practitioner, with some notes on how to use it.

Draft contract of employment for ancillary staff

Part I of this statement sets out particulars of the terms and conditions agreed between

I/We, Dr(s) .... (name)
of .... (address)
and you .... (name)
.... (address)
on .... (date)

Part II of this statement sets out information on the disciplinary procedure, whom you should contact if you wish to appeal against a disciplinary decision or to take up a grievance, and the subsequent steps to be followed in the disciplinary and grievance procedure.

Your employment with me began on. . . .
Your employment with your previous employer does not count as part of your continuous period of employment.

Part I

Job title

(1) Receptionist.

Salary

(2) Your salary is . . . per annum, payable in arrears on . . . every month, and your equivalent hourly rate is. . . .
London Weighting Allowance is also payable at the appropriate level to those staff covered by agreements of the Administrative and Clerical Staffs Whitley Council. The agreement may be seen at. . . . Your salary is reviewed annually.

Incremental date

Your incremental date is . . . and payment of your first increment is due on. . . .

Hours of work

(3) Your basic hours of work at 36 per week, your normal hours of attendance are. .... (A detailed account of a rota arrangement may be required here.) In addition to these hours occasional Saturday morning surgeries will have to be covered on a rotation basis; an arrangement in which all members of staff are required to participate. The salary is calculated to allow for this extra duty and no overtime payments for this session will be made. Staff will be required to work overtime occasionally at the request of a doctor— for example, when colleagues are on holiday or are ill, extra hours may have to be worked to cover the opening time of the surgery.

Overtime payment

Additional overtime payment will then be made at the rate normally paid for an hour's work.

Annual leave

(4) You are entitled to four weeks' paid annual leave, which is normally taken between Easter and Christmas of each year. Reasonable notice must be given of your intention to take leave, and all leave must be arranged with the doctor in charge so that there is adequate cover for the surgery.

Leave must be taken by the end of the calendar year and may not be accumulated from one year to the next unless by prior agreement. Leave entitlement is calculated at the rate of one-twelfth of a full year's entitlement for each month of completed service during the first year of employment or during the year of resignation—for example, 3 February to 1 March would equal one month. If a member of staff has anticipated his or her leave entitlement before termination an appropriate deduction may be made from any payment owing.

Bank holidays

The surgery will be closed on official bank and public holidays and any proclaimed National holidays.

Sick leave

(5) If you are entitled to statutory sick pay this will be paid by the employer.

Your entitlement under the employer's own sick pay scheme

(which may be revised or withdrawn at his discretion) in any 12 month period is as follows:

Period of continuous service	Basic salary*	Basic half salary*
Less than 6 months	Nil	Nil
6 months to 12 months	Nil	1 month
13 months to 2 years	1 month	2 months
3 years to 5 years	2 months	2 months
Over 5 years	2 months	4 months

Any payment under the Statutory Sick Pay Scheme will be offset against your entitlement under the employer's scheme.

Notification of absence due to sickness must be made as early as possible on the first day of sickness. If the absence continues beyond seven working days a medical certificate should be submitted. A self certification form should be completed for any sickness absence lasting for seven days or less. If the illness lasts for more than seven calendar days you must first notify your absence and also request a self certification form which should be posted to the practice at the end of the first week of absence.

Any accident or injury arising out of your employment must be reported immediately to the doctor on duty.

*If you are entitled to receive any National Insurance benefits the following deductions will be made from an allowance equal to full basic salary, irrespective of whether you register a claim. So you are advised to ensure that you claim all your entitlements under these Acts.

(a) The amounts of sickness or invalidity benefits recoverable under National Insurance Acts, if appropriate.

(b) The amount of injury benefit receivable under the National (Industrial Injuries) Act, if appropriate.

(c) The amount of earnings related supplement to sickness and injury benefit receivable under the National Insurance Acts, if appropriate.

Maternity leave

(6) Subject to her length of service and certain other conditions as laid down in the Employment Protection (Consolidation) Act 1978 and subsequent amending legislation, and the Social Security Act 1986, women on the staff are entitled to statutory maternity pay and to return to a job. A certificate of confinement and due notice in writing of maternity absence and return to work, or both, should be provided as required in the Acts.

Pension scheme

(7) Give details, if any. (There are no pension rights attaching to this employment and there is no contracting out certificate in force under the Social Security Pensions Act 1975.)

Notice of termination of employment

(8) You are required to give written notice of your intention to

31

terminate your employment and you are entitled to receive in writing the same minimum period of notice. This period of notice is calculated as follows:

You are entitled to receive one week's notice of termination, increasing to two weeks after two years' service. Thereafter your notice entitlement and requirement will increase by one week for each additional complete year of service up to a maximum of 12 weeks for 12 years' service or longer.

By mutual agreement the period of notice may be varied. Payment in lieu of notice may be made.

Health and safety at work

(9) The practice's policy on health and safety at work is to provide as safe and healthy working conditions as possible and to enlist the support of their employees towards achieving these ends.

While the overall responsibility rests with your employer, all staff have a legal duty to take reasonable care to avoid injury to themselves or to others by their work activities, and not to interfere with or misuse any clothing or equipment provided to protect health and safety.

The main hazards that staff should be aware of are: *(i)* medical instruments, etc, in the consulting room; *(ii)* prams, bicycles, etc.

Any accident to a member of staff or a member of the public should be reported to the doctor in charge immediately. A factual statement covering to the fullest possible extent all the circumstances of the accident may be required to ascertain the cause to prevent its recurrence.

Part II

Disciplinary procedure

Preamble

Disciplinary rules and procedures are necessary for promoting fairness and order in the treatment of individuals. They also assist a practice to operate effectively. Rules set standards of conduct and performance at work; procedure helps to ensure that the standards are adhered to and also provides a fair method of dealing with alleged failures to observe them.

Disciplinary procedures should not be viewed primarily as a means of imposing sanctions. They should also be designed to emphasise and encourage improvements in individual conduct.

Individuals will be informed of the complaints against them and be given an opportunity to state their case before decisions are reached. They have a right to be accompanied by a colleague at all stages in the procedure. Any warning given in this procedure will be deemed to have lapsed after one year, subject to satisfactory conduct.

The following disciplinary procedure will apply:

Counselling—If there is thought to be cause for action under this disciplinary procedure, you will first be asked to attend to discuss the matter with the doctor in charge. The proceedings will not be recorded. It is hoped that this informal counselling will resolve any possible difficulties and lead to the required improvement.

Verbal warning—If following this there is continued cause for concern, there will be a further meeting with the doctor in charge. You will have an opportunity to state your case. You may be accompanied by a colleague. If following this disciplinary action is deemed appropriate a verbal warning will be given. The warning will state the nature of the misconduct, specify the disciplinary action being taken, indicate the likely consequences of committing misconduct again, and state, if appropriate, the period of time given for improvement.

Written warning—If following this there is continued cause for concern, a formal written warning will be given by the doctor in charge stating the nature of the complaint and that if no improvement is forthcoming it may result in your dismissal.

Dismissal—If there is no improvement you may then be dismissed.

Appeal—Where circumstances permit, the right of appeal against dismissal should be to a doctor who has not been directly involved.

Serious misconduct—There are varying degrees of seriousness of misconduct, so this procedure may be started at any stage depending on the severity of the misconduct. A few examples of gross misconduct that would justify summary dismissal without prior warning are theft, abuse of medicines, and serious breach of confidentiality. In some circumstances where serious misconduct is thought to have occurred, the member of staff concerned may be

33

suspended on full basic salary pending an investigation and a hearing.

Grievance procedure

If you have any grievance relating to your employment you should raise this with Dr. ... Minor grievances may be raised orally, but serious grievances must be in writing.

Signed .... for the employer

This ..... day of 19

I acknowledge receipt of this contract of employment and agree to be bound by it. I understand that you retained a copy of this signed contract.

Signed .... employee

This ..... day of 19

Notes of guidance on the draft contract of employment

(1) Date of contract—Fill in date when Contract is signed. The date employment begins, for example, is important because various employment rights depend on continuity of service. The date must therefore take account of any employment with a previous employer that counts towards a period of continuous employment by the present employer.

(2) Employer—The full name and address of the employer(s) should appear in this space. Contracts should not be provided for staff who are in fact employed by someone other than the practitioner, such as area health authority staff attached to a practice.

(3) Title of job—It is important that this should adequately describe the scope of the employee's job as the employee otherwise may be justified in maintaining that work which he or she is asked to do is inconsistent with the job.

(4) The provisions of a Contract with regard to the previous period of employment are important whenever the employee has been in the practice longer than the employer(s); because under the Employment Protection (Consolidation) Act 1978 and the Transfer of Undertakings (Protection of Employment) Regula-

tions 1981 when a practice is transferred from one doctor to another, the period of employment of an employee in the practice at the time of the transfer would normally count as a period of employment with the transferee and the transfer shall not break the continuity of the period of employment.

Thus, whereas a practitioner who takes on a new employee will incur very few obligations during the first two years, it is only at the end of this period that, for example, she becomes entitled to compensation if she is unfairly dismissed unless the dismissal is for an inadmissible reason. But if the employer takes over a practice in which the employee has already worked for 10 years, then even on the second day of the practice the employer will not be able to dismiss her without paying compensation based on the full 10 years' employment.

(5) Holidays—The parties are free to make their own arrangements in this regard. In small practices one of the most frequent sources of difficulty concerns staff who are unable to arrange their holidays so that they do not coincide. The form suggests one way in which this difficulty may be met, an alternative solution is to provide that in the event of such coincidence the employer shall decide when the holiday will be taken.

(6) Sickness or injury—Apart from Statutory Sick Pay, employment legislation does not require the employer to pay any statutory minimum in respect of periods of sickness or injury. An industrial tribunal would, however, endorse any right which the employer acquires under a Contract of Employment.

(7) Pensions—Some practices run their own pension schemes: if they do and if a contracting out certificate is in force then the Contract should say so.

(8) Notice—The periods of notice recommended are the statutory minima.

(9) Discipline—The Act provides that the Contract of Employment should tell an employee where details of the disciplinary procedure and rules governing an appeal against disciplinary action are to be found.

(10) Grievance procedure—The Act provides that the Contract of Employment must describe the grievance procedure.

Job description

This should normally be a separate and distinct document from the Contract itself. It should set out the main task of the job, but also include the mundane tasks—for example, making tea—which employees sometimes prefer to forget or neglect.

IV: Can I still dismiss?

Many employers, particularly those with only a handful of staff, are fearful about the prospects of dismissing staff. Some even believe that the right to dismiss has been taken away from them by current employment legislation. This is not true. An employer still has the right to dismiss an employee, but if the procedure adopted and the reasons for the dismissal are not demonstrably fair then substantial compensation may be awarded to the employee.

Poor management

In fact it is usually the employer who has neglected his management responsibilities who is at risk of being involved in an unfair dismissal case. Many of the difficulties that doctors experience with ancillary staff originate from an unsatisfactory approach to their selection, recruitment, training and supervision. A brief reminder of these responsibilities may be helpful. Firstly, at the outset, when a new member of staff is recruited, it is essential to have an accurate job description and to adopt a proper procedure for the interview and selection. Secondly, when an offer of a job is made both the doctor and the employee should be aware of the importance of the probationary period. Its length may vary, but I would recommend nine months. This allows sufficient time to train and assess a new employee, and is well before the completion of two years' service, the point after which important individual employment rights begin to apply.

The probationary period is crucial. But before we start thinking of what action may be required to improve performance in the job, a new member of the staff should be told what is required and given every encouragement and assistance to do the job satisfactorily. Many employers seem to forget the obvious and essential need to explain to new staff what is required of them. If this is done and performance then falls below the required standard, steps must be taken to inform the employee of this and to encourage him or her to improve. At each stage a written record must be kept for future reference, and if the point is reached when it seems that satisfactory performance cannot be achieved, than the employee should be informed in writing that the probationary period cannot be confirmed. This approach should be relatively easy to adopt for the doctor who employs only a handful of staff. Each step is logical and easy to follow. And it should minimise the risk of having to dismiss staff. In short, each employer should have a recognised procedure for handling disciplinary matters and grievances, and what has been decribed here is in fact the outline of such a procedure.

If, even after following this procedure, having taken all the necessary steps to ensure that newly recruited staff are satisfactory, it subsequently transpires that an employee who was previously satisfactory is no longer so, or that a serious offence is committed that requires disciplinary action, the doctor has the right ultimately to dismiss. But care must be taken to follow closely to the disciplinary procedure as stated in the contract of employment, and to keep a written record of the action that is taken.

Unsatisfactory staff

Undoubtedly, a few general practitioners employ staff whose performance is well below the standard required. This is probably a legacy of previous neglect of their responsibilities as employers— a casual approach to recruitment, inadequate training and supervision, and the probationary period has been omitted from the contract. The point has been reached where something should be done, but none of the partners has either the courage or the inclination to do anything. Often the BMA member will turn to the BMA Regional Office for advice.

Although the position of staff who are unsatisfactory but have had long service with the practice is always difficult to resolve, it is not irretrievable. It must be remembered that the difficulty has been largely caused by inadequate management by the doctor, and great care will need to be taken if it is decided to proceed with disciplinary action, which may end in dismissal. The employee who has been working unsatisfactorily, often for many years, has strong grounds for arguing that his or her performance could be *presumed* to be satisfactory simply because no one had expressed any view to the contrary. The industrial tribunals almost invariably interpret the lack of any criticism from the employer as a reasonable basis for an employee presuming that his work was satisfactory. Thus the doctor's laudable efforts to retrieve a situation that has been allowed to drift for years and to act in accordance with his responsibilities as a manager may at first meet with considerable difficulties and require the advice and assistance of those who are well experienced in these matters.

What does dismissal mean?

Employees have the right not to be unfairly dismissed. Any employee who thinks he has been unfairly dismissed may seek a remedy by complaining to an industrial tribunal. Before a claim for unfair dismissal can be heard by a tribunal, the employee must establish that dismissal took place. Dismissal occurs when: (a) the employer terminates the contract with or without notice; (b) a fixed-term contract expires without being renewed (a claim cannot be made if the contract is for one year or more and the employee has previously agreed in writing to forego his right of complaint); (c) the employee resigns in cases where the employer's conduct shows intention not to be bound by the terms of the contract of employment or where the employer has broken a fundamental term of contract of employment. This is often described as "constructive dismissal", and occurs when the treatment of an employee by the employer is so unpleasant or intolerable that the employee feels compelled to resign.

Those who cannot complain of unfair dismissal

The general rule is that employees who have not completed two years' continuous employment with their employer, or who have reached normal retiring age for their employment (or if there is no normal retiring age, have reached 65 for both men and women) cannot complain of unfair dismissal. (Prior to 1 June 1985 any employee working for an employer with 21 or more staff had the right to complain of unfair dismissal after one year of service. This qualifying period has been extended to two years.)

There is, however, no qualifying period of employment or age limit for those complaining of unfair dismissal on account of trade union membership or activities.

Fair and unfair dismissal

Dismissal can only be fair if the employer can show that the reason for it was one of these:
—a reason related to the employee's capability or qualification for the job;
—a reason related to the employee's conduct;
—redundancy;
—a statutory duty or restriction that prevents the employment being continued;
—some other substantial reason that could justify the dismissal. The employer must also show that he acted reasonably in the circumstances in treating that reason as sufficient to justify dismissing the employee. But the tribunal will take account of the size and administrative resources of the employer's undertaking.

Dismissal for redundancy may be unfair if the employee was unfairly selected for redundancy. Dismissal on account of pregnancy will, in most cases, also be unfair and may not require a two year qualifying period. Dismissal will also normally be unfair when it is for being a member of or for taking part in the activities of an independent trade union, or for not being a member of a trade union which is not independent.

Remedies for unfair dismissal

There are three possible remedies for unfair dismissal:
—reinstatement (the employee is to be treated in all respects as though the dismissal has not occurred);
—re-engagement (the employee is to be re-employed but not necessarily in the same job or on the same terms and conditions of employment);
—compensation, up to a maximum award in normal circumstances of over £20 000.

Written statement of the reasons for dismissal

Employees who have been dismissed and who have completed six months' employment have the right to receive from their employers on request a written statement of the reasons for dismissal.

Individual employment rights

Right	Principal legislation	Eligibility (length of service)
(1) To be given a minimum period of notice—based on length of service—of termination of employment	Employment Protection (Consolidation) Act 1978	1 month
(2) To be given written particulars of terms of employment .. .. .. ;	"	Immediately (the employer has* 13 weeks in which to supply it)
(3) To receive equal pay with a member of the opposite sex doing similar work .	Equal Pay Act 1970	Immediately
(4) Not to be discriminated against on the grounds of marriage or sex	Sex Discrimination Act 1975	Any stage from advertising of job
(5) Not to be discriminated against on the grounds of colour, race, nationality, or ethnic or national origins	Race Relations Act 1976	Any stage from advertising of job
(6) Not to be unfairly dismissed	Employment Protection (Consolidation) Act 1978 and Employment Act 1980	2 years*†
(7) To receive a guaranteed payment when no work is available	Employment Protection (Consolidation) Act 1978	1 month*
(8) To receive payment when suspended on medical grounds—in certain specified industries only	"	1 month
(9) Not to be dismissed on pregnancy grounds	"	2 years or immediately if regarded as sex discrimination*

No.	Right	Act	Qualification
(10)	To receive payment for absence due to pregnancy or maternity	Social Security Act 1986	26 weeks
(11)	To return to work after absence due to pregnancy or maternity leave	Employment Protection (Consolidation) Act 1978	2 years
(12)	Not to have action—short of dismissal—taken against him/her because of trade union membership or activity	"	Immediately
(13)	To have time off—with pay—for carrying out trade union duties or for approved industrial relations training, if trade union is recognised for collective bargaining purposes	"	Immediately
(14)	To have time off for trade union activities if trade union is recognised for collective bargaining purposes	"	Immediately
(15)	To have time off for public duties	"	Immediately
(16)	To have time off—with pay—to seek alternative work or to arrange training in a redundancy situation	"	2 years*
(17)	To have protection in case of employer's insolvency	"	Immediately
(18)	To receive on request a written statement of the reason for dismissal	"	6 months* (will be increased to 2 years)
(19)	To receive an itemised pay statement	"	Immediately
(20)	To have paid time off for antenatal care	Employment Act 1980	Immediately
(21)	To have a protected period of notice and for his trade union—where recognised by his employer for collective bargaining purposes—to be consulted in a redundancy situation	Employment Protection Act 1975	Immediately

Note: *Employees working 16 hours or more per week are eligible. After 5 years' continuous employment, employees working 8 hours or more a week are eligible. †If dismissal is for certain inadmissable reasons—that is, for reasons of trade union membership or activities—there is no length of service qualification.

(BMA copyright)

Employers are required to comply with an employee's request for such a statement within 14 days of the request being made.

A final note of reassurance

For the most part, employers rarely experience the problem of dismissing staff. Most staff are loyal and provide a very high standard of service. No problems have ever arisen or are likely to arise in the future. In such circumstances where there is an entirely happy and satisfactory working relationship the doctor should be most careful not to upset it by providing contracts of employment where none have been supplied previously. The sudden and unexpected introduction of a degree of formality into the working relationship could so easily be misunderstood. So do please consider the possible psychological impact on your staff of any action you may decide to take.

How to change a contract of employment

Employment contracts are continually changing and developing. Every pay rise requires a variation of the original contract, as does any change in the duties or hours of work of the staff. Although your staff may be tolerant of change as such (especially if they benefit from it), some variations in their contracts may meet with strong objections and even resistance.

Some general practitioners have come to believe that they cannot change a contract of employment once it has been agreed with an employee. Others think that because it is a written contract then change is even more difficult to achieve, and in some cases even take this view as justification for not providing written contracts of employment. In fact any employer can change an employee's contract, but he may find himself in serious difficulties if he approaches it in the wrong way.

Nature of the employment contract

It may be helpful to begin by reminding ourselves what constitutes a contract of employment. Firstly, it is important to remember that a contract exists between you and your employees irrespective of whether most of it has been encapsulated in a written document. Moreover, even if there is a comprehensive written document the contract of employment when viewed in its entirety also includes unwritten understandings and working practices (which are commonly referred to as "custom and practice").

The law requires you to issue to any employees working more than 16 hours a week a statement of the main particulars of employment. (This must also be issued to any employee working for more than eight hours a week who has been employed by you for five years.) The written statement should be issued within 13 weeks of the employee starting work and should include the following information:

(1) Name of the parties
(2) Date employment began and statement about continuity
(3) Job title
(4) Pay
(5) Hours
(6) Holiday and holiday pay provisions
(7) Sick pay
(8) Pension
(9) Notice
(10) Grievance, disciplinary, and appeals procedures.

The law requires that changes in the terms of the main particulars of employment need to be notified to the employee within one month of the change.

In addition, the law requires an employer of five or more staff to issue a written statement of his general policy on health and safety matters as these affect his staff and the arrangements that he has made for carrying out his policy.

The statutory requirement to provide written statements on these matters does not have to be supplemented in any way. There is no legal obligation to provide a written contract as such. But in practice the written statement of the main particulars of employment (together with your policy statement on health and safety matters) can be regarded as the basis of a written contract of employment. The contract as a whole also includes the job description (whether written or not) and the many informal understandings and working practices which always form an important part of any employment contract. An example of these informal and unwritten practices are the arrangements normally followed when staff take coffee and tea breaks, including allocating the duty of actually making coffee or tea for the general practitioner and his partners.

Need for consent

In practice there are various approaches to changing a contract of employment. Whichever approach is adopted the basic principle that must be borne in mind is that an employee should consent to changes before these can become contractually binding, irrespective of whether the consent is implied or by express agreement, given in advance of or at the time of the change. This principle underlies the different ways in which employment terms may be changed.

It is always preferable, if possible, to seek to reach agreement on the proposed changes. Of course, many employees are not favourably disposed towards changes of any kind, particularly if these affect their duties or hours of work. But sometimes you may be surprised at their receptiveness. Secondly, it is very important to give clear and defensible reasons for the change. Try to explain why it is necessary in the interests of the good running of the practice. Try to ensure that your reasons are fully understood (even if they are not initially accepted) and never rely on other members of your staff to put your case on your behalf. Often there is nothing more damaging than a second hand explanation of your intentions, particularly if it is given by someone who is not favourably disposed towards them. Most general practitioners work with a small enough group of staff for this personal approach to be practicable.

When you have explained the change, and your reasons for having to introduce it, listen carefully to any reasons your staff may have for not accepting it. It is worth considering carefully how far their objections can be answered. If their reasons for not wanting the change seem reasonable it is well worth taking the time and trouble to examine them to see whether a compromise can be agreed which will satisfy both the needs of your practice and the wishes of your staff. At this point you may even find yourself participating in some gentle and informal negotiations. A compromise is often possible and well worth looking for at the outset of the whole exercise. If you aim at a compromise this may lead you to increase marginally the extent of your original proposals, if only to enable you to show your own willingness to compromise.

If your staff consent to your proposed changes

The crucial consideration when changing an employment contract is the matter of "consent," and this can be given by an employee in various ways.

(i) Consent given by express agreement

This may be given verbally, but to avoid problems of proof and disputes about who said what and when, it is preferable to obtain such agreement in writing. An employer is, in any case, required to put in writing the term of the contract (as changed) if it relates to any one of those matters listed above.

If your employee has expressly consented to the change there is usually no doubt that the new term of the contract is contractually binding. It is important to bear in mind that there is a difference between a position where your employee voluntarily accepts a new term and one where it is effectively imposed because the option of declining the proposed change is not a practical possibility. As you may expect, this matter turns on the question of what may be regarded as "reasonable." There are no hard and fast rules which can be applied here. What is and is not "reasonable" depends on the nature of the change, your reasons for introducing it, and the circumstances in which it is being implemented.

(ii) Consent shown by implied agreement

Implied agreement is normally assumed if your employee continues to work under the new contractual terms without complaint. In fact it can be established by custom and practice if all the employees affected by the change are fully aware of it and continue to work. For this reason it is most important for an employee to make known any objection without delay and to ensure that the objection is clearly understood by the employer.

Your written contracts can allow for change

The contract itself may contain provisions that allow for changes in such matters as pay, the place of work, working hours, and the duties of the job. In these circumstances the actual change is a matter for the general practitioner to initiate as the employer and manager. This arrangement typically applies if the pay of your staff is increased annually as a consequence of pay settlements elsewhere in the health service.

The way in which change can be allowed for within the terms of a written contract is by "broad" drafting. For example, a receptionist's contract may say that her pay is to be determined by reference to a document setting out the rates of pay for National

Health Service clerical and administrative staff. Similarly, the contract might state that the receptionist is required to work at the partner's premises, wherever these may be located in the practice area. In the job description reference may be made to "any other duties of a clerical or administrative nature that may be required from time to time."

The overall effect of drafting the contract in this way is to increase your rights, as the employer and manager of your staff, to alter your employees' duties, to change the location where they work, and even to vary their hours and shifts. Of course, on the other side of the equation, there is a corresponding loss of rights for your staff.

It is particularly important to note that the job descriptions of your staff, their hours of work, and their place of work are three aspects of their contracts that should be written in a manner which allows for change. It is too easy for people to presume that the ambit of their contract obligations is the same as the duties they actually perform. This may happen if staff become accustomed to a more limited range of duties than those originally defined in their contracts and may be avoided if their job descriptions are broadly drafted.

If you have taken care to draft broadly this does not mean that you have an unfettered right to vary your employees' contracts as you wish. If your change leads to the sacking of an employee you may find that the industrial tribunal, in considering an unfair dismissal claim, will wish to examine whether the change you introduced was reasonable in all the circumstances.

If consent is not forthcoming

It may not be possible to obtain the consent of your staff even if you have made considerable efforts to agree the change with them. At this stage if you decide to go ahead and implement the change you should give reasonable notice of your intentions. Ultimately, if you are called to defend your actions in an industrial tribunal they will be concerned about the extent to which you have consulted your staff and sought to reach agreement with them and the reasonableness of your changes in the contracts of employment. Fortunately, these tribunals recognise that any business has to be run efficiently, that no business arrangements can remain static and immutable, and that we live in a world where change is regarded as an essential prerequisite for survival.

In normal circumstances any change imposed unilaterally by an employer without the consent of the employee will be a breach of contract. If this is a *fundamental* breach of contract, hitting at the heart of the contract, the employee may be entitled to claim compensation for constructive dismissal. Furthermore, even if it does not constitute a fundamental breach an employee can claim damages for the breach in a civil court. It is possible (but not always so) to avoid these problems if you give sufficient notice of your intention to introduce the change. It has been thought that the length of notice of the change required is the same as that which would be needed to terminate the contract lawfully. But even if this length of notice is given the employer could be liable to pay compensation for unfair dismissal or redundancy if the employee still refuses to accept the change and subsequently leaves. The advantage of giving adequate notice of the change is that your employees are likely to be left with little or no time to protest after the change has been introduced because they have already had time to think it over.

A written contract is advisable

The chapter on "employment law" emphasises the benefits of having properly documented written contracts of employment for your staff. In particular, I recommended general practitioners to satisfy their legal obligations by issuing to their staff written statements of the main terms and conditions of service. It is important to remember that a contract of employment exists between you and your staff irrespective of whether it has been expressed in writing. The industrial tribunals will not hesitate to interpret and clarify the terms of an unwritten contract by drawing on a knowledge of your verbal understandings and the customs and practices associated with your surgery and its staff. The advantage of a written contract, if it is properly drafted, is that it clarifies beyond any reasonable doubt the terms of service of your staff, including their duties and their hours of work. Furthermore, if the contract is carefully drafted (as suggested above) it can allow you to introduce changes without the risk of incurring serious legal difficulties.

There are some general practitioners who have provided their staff with written contracts and now believe that it is difficult, if not impossible, to change these. It must be emphasised that the issues in changing the terms of an employment contract are essentially the same irrespective of whether it is based primarily on a formal written agreement or simply consists of verbal agreements, understandings, and customary working practices. It is only the practicalities that may differ.

When deciding how to approach the business of varying a contract of employment it is vital to recognise that there are no firm guidelines on what is reasonable or unreasonable. We can only point to general principles which are largely derived from the case law of industrial tribunals and the courts.

Finally, there is an important adage which should always be borne in mind at the outset: you must never assume before you start that changes cannot be made. Too often employers are debilitated by their own defeatist attitudes and consequently do not even begin to consider the options available to them.

I am grateful to Dr John Ball and Dr Ewen Bramwell for their advice. I am, of course, responsible for any omissions or errors.

Rights of the expectant mother

Most practices employ only a handful of staff and a high proportion are women. The employment rights of the expectant mother are both intricate and stringent. Thus any employer with few staff may be faced with serious administrative difficulties if a member of staff is pregnant.

It is probably not widely realised that the expectant mother does not have a right to maternity leave as such. This needs to be said because it helps to clarify the four employment rights that are acquired by an expectant mother: (*i*) not to be unreasonably refused time off work for antenatal care and to be paid when permitted that time off; (*ii*) to complain of unfair dismissal because of pregnancy; (*iii*) to receive statutory maternity pay; (*iv*) to return to work with her employer after a period of absence on account of pregnancy or confinement.

These rights are acquired by all women employees, married or unmarried, but they are subject to the conditions and limitations described below. It should be noted that these rights do not apply to women who are independent contractors.

The following account of the law governing maternity rights is complex. It is intended to serve as a source document to be referred to when the need arises. It is important to note at the outset that there are different qualifying conditions for each of the maternity rights. For example, any employee has the right to take paid time off work for antenatal care irrespective of how long she has been employed, whereas the right to complain of unfair dismissal is acquired only after two years of employment.

Because this area of employment law is complex you should not hesitate to seek expert advice and assistance. BMA members may seek help from their BMA regional office.

Time off for antenatal care

Irrespective of how long she has worked in your practice an employee has the right not to be unreasonably refused time off work to receive antenatal care and to be paid for this time off. To acquire this right the following conditions have to be met. Firstly, she must have made an appointment for antenatal care and the time off must be requested to keep the appointment. Secondly, except in the case of the request for time off for the first appointment, the employee must if asked produce for your inspection both a certificate from a medical practitioner, midwife, or health visitor stating that she is pregnant and an appointment card (or some other document) showing that the appointment has been made. Your employee should be paid the appropriate hourly rate for the period of absence from work. Any employee who is improperly denied these rights is entitled to complain to a tribunal. These rights are acquired by any woman as soon as she joins your staff.

Right to complain of unfair dismissal

Subject to the qualifying conditions described below an employee has the right to complain of unfair dismissal if her employer dismisses her because she is pregnant or for a reason connected with her pregnancy. Except in the circumstances stated below such a dismissal will be *automatically unfair*; in other words, as the employer there are no grounds on which you may defend your action.

In general, a woman must have been continuously employed for at least two years if she normally works for 16 or more hours a week, or if she normally works for eight to 16 hours a week, for at least five years. In most circumstances there should be no doubt whether or not an employee has worked for long enough to acquire the right to complain of unfair dismissal, to receive maternity pay, or to return to work after confinement. But if there is a change in the partnership, or if a practice is "transferred" to another practice, these events do not normally interrupt the employee's continuity of employment.

There are exceptional circumstances where dismissal for reasons of pregnancy may not necessarily be unfair. These are where the woman's condition makes it impossible to do the job adequately or

51

if it would be against the law for her to do that particular job while pregnant. Because the likelihood of these circumstances arising in general practice is fairly remote they are not discussed in detail here. But you must offer the employee a suitable alternative job if one is available, and you should seek immediate advice from your BMA regional office if you foresee this situation arising.

The legal status of maternity leave

Because this is both intricate and important, and there is so much confusion about it, it is essential to spell out the precise legal status of maternity leave. The Employment Protection (Consolidation) Act 1978 and the Social Security Act 1986 do *not* create a right to maternity leave as such. Nor do they even require an employer to pay the employee her salary as such or to give her any of the other benefits of her contract of employment while she is absent from work because of pregnancy or confinement. These are matters to be agreed between you and your employee and should be encapsulated in your written contract of employment. But what the legislation does create—and this is important—is the right for a women to receive *statutory maternity pay* (as distinct from salary) to be paid by her employer during the intitial stages of her absence (whether or not she is still in your employment) and the right to return to work. Both of these rights are subject to important limitations and these are explained below.

Right to statutory maternity pay

Once your employee has stopped work, she is entitled to receive statutory maternity pay (SMP), if she satisfies certain qualifying conditions, regardless of whether she intends to return.

SMP is payable for 18 weeks from any date between the eleventh and sixth week before the expected week of confinement. The normal qualifying conditions are:
(i) 26 weeks' continuous employment;
(ii) normal weekly earnings not less than the National Insurance (NI) lower limit, currently £43 per week;
(iii) 21 days' prior notice of intended absence;
(iv) still be pregnant at the eleventh week before expected week of confinement.

Employees paying reduced rate NI contributions, part timers and "casual" or temporary staff are all entitled to SMP if they satisfy these conditions.

Other important features of SMP are:

(i) Two rates are payable; a higher rate for the first six weeks for employees with at least two years' continuous employment [or five years' if working between eight and 16 hours a week], and a lower rate which replaces the NI maternity allowance.

(ii) An employee can ask for independent social security adjudication to determine any dispute over payment of SMP.

(iii) Special SMP arrangements apply to premature births, dismissals during pregnancy, and an employer's insolvency.

(iv) The employer can recover the full cost of SMP payments and the NI contributions payable on them from the Department of Social Security.

(v) You can choose to pay a level of maternity pay higher than the eligible SMP rate.

Because of the basic requirements, women who have recently changed jobs are often ineligible for SMP. However, any woman who cannot satisfy SMP requirements, but has substantial previous employment, may be entitled to be paid statutory maternity allowance (SMA).

No employer can avoid his or her liability to pay SMP if the qualifying conditions are met. But it may be paid as part of a larger payment which includes the employer's own maternity pay.

There are two rates of SMP:

(i) A higher rate which is 90% of the employee's average weekly earnings, which is payable for the first six weeks of the maternity pay period.

(ii) A lower rate for the remaining weeks, normally 12.

To qualify for the higher rate, an employee must satisfy all the normal qualifying conditions and must also have been continuously employed for at least two years by the fifteenth week before the expected week of confinement for normally 16 hours or more a week, or for five years for normally eight hours a week.

The legislation provides for two principal "easements":

(i) Any continuous period of employment for at least two years for 16 hours or more a week, followed by a further period of working eight to 16 hours a week ending with the fifteenth week before the expected confinement gives an entitlement to higher rate SMP.

(ii) Any continuous period of two years' employment normally for 16 hours or more a week, but including up to 26 weeks working only eight–16 hours will also count for SMP.

The lower rate of SMP is payable for the remainder of the maternity pay period (normally 12 weeks) after six weeks at the higher rate, or for the whole 18 weeks if the employee is not entitled to the higher rate.

The central feature of SMP is that it is paid by the employer and not the Department of Social Security, like statutory sick pay. SMP is subject to PAYE deductions for NI contributions and income tax, though there should not be any liability on lower rate SMP alone because this rate is below NI and tax thresholds. Finally, other deductions (such as pension contributions) can also be made from SMP.

Further information is available from your local DSS office; ask for leaflet NI 257 *Employer's Guide to SMP*.

Right to come back to work

The law gives an employee the right (subject to the limitations outlined below) to her former job at any time before the end of the period of 29 weeks (a week normally means a week ending with Saturday) beginning with the week in which her child is born (the 29 week period may in some circumstances be extended) and on her return to be employed on terms no less favourable than those that would have applied to her if she had not been absent. For example, if your staff had received a pay increase during her absence this would also have to be applied to her.

Several conditions have to be met to acquire this right:

(1) Your employee must have been continuously employed by you for at least two years immediately before the beginning of the eleventh week, before the expected week of confinement if she normally works for 16 or more hours a week, or for at least five years if she normally works for eight to 16 hours a week.

(2) Your employee must continue to be employed by you (whether or not she is actually coming to work) until immediately before the beginning of the eleventh week before the expected week of confinement.

(3) Your employee must give the following information to you *in writing* at least 21 days before she begins her maternity absence (or if this is not possible, as soon as is reasonably practicable): (*a*)

that she is away from work to have a baby; (b) that she intends to return to work after this absence; (c) the expected week of confinement (if the confinement has already occurred the date of confinement).

(4) If you asked for a certificate of the expected week of confinement this must be produced.

After the maternity absence has begun the following conditions apply:

(1) You may send her a written request, not earlier than 49 days from the date you were notified as the beginning of the expected week of confinement, asking her to confirm in writing that she intends to return to work. If you write asking for this confirmation you should explain in your letter that she must give confirmation in writing within 14 days of receiving your letter. Again, if this is not possible her confirmation should be given as soon as is reasonably practicable. If she does not reply confirming her intention to return the right to return is lost.

(2) She must inform you in writing of the date she intends to return at least 21 days before that date. (The Department of Employment has provided examples of completed written notifications—see appendix.)

Return to work

Your employee may choose when to return to work, provided that it is within a period of 29 weeks beginning with the week in which her child was born. If she is ill and produces a medical certificate she may delay her return for a further four weeks from the date she originally gave for her return, or, if she has not notified a date, for up to four weeks from the end of the 29 week period. She may, however, delay her return to work only once. You may defer an employee's return to work for up to four weeks from her notified date provided that you give specified reasons and inform the employee of the date on which she may return.

If you do not allow your employee to return to her old job this will be treated as dismissal. Her right to return, however, may be restricted in the following circumstances:

(1) If the total number of your employees immediately before the beginning of her maternity absence was five or less, and you can show that it is not reasonably practicable for you to take her back in her old job (or to offer her suitable alternative work—

which means work that is both suitable and appropriate for the employee, and where the terms, conditions, and location are not substantially less favourable than those of the old job) the failure to permit her return will not be treated as a dismissal and any claim of unfair dismissal will fail. But if these circumstances occur the onus of proof lies with the employer.

(2) If her former job in the practice is no longer available because of redundancy the Act states you must offer her a suitable alternative job if one is available, otherwise the dismissal will be automatically unfair. If she unreasonably refuses a suitable offer, however, she may lose her right to redundancy pay.

(3) If you can show that it is not reasonably practicable, for a reason other than redundancy, to offer your employee her old job back, that you have offered a suitable alternative job, and that the employee has subsequently unreasonably rejected the offer (or even accepted it on unreasonable terms) your failure to permit her return to her original job will not be treated as a dismissal and any claim of unfair dismissal will fail. In these circumstances the onus of proof lies with you as the employer.

Finally, if you employ a temporary replacement you must inform her in writing that her employment will be terminated on the return of your employee who is absent because of pregnancy or confinement.

Legal labyrinth

This area of employment law must surely be most complex for both the employer and employee. I cannot personally apologise for its complexity because I have had no responsibility for its drafting or its content. For the employer with only a handful of staff, without a personnel manager or personnel department, applying the law requires care. Any mistake, even if it is wholly due to ignorance or a misunderstanding of the law, could lead to a tribunal case and even a costly award against you. Indeed, it is almost a test of tenacity for both you and your employee to satisfy the requirements of the employment rights of the expectant mother.

I am grateful to Dr John Ball, Dr Ewen Bramwell, and Mr Peter Syson and his colleagues of ACAS for their comments on this paper. I am, of course, responsible for any omissions or errors.

Appendix

Examples of written notifications on the right to return

(1)   Employee's first notification: to be given to the employer at least 21 days before beginning maternity absence (or, if it is not reasonably practicable to do so by that date, as soon as is reasonably practicable afterwards).

Dear Mr Other,
This is to let you know that
1   I am leaving work to have a baby
2   My expected week of confinement is . . . .
3   I intend to return to work after the baby is born.
                          Yours sincerely,
                            Ophelia X

(2)   Employer's request for confirmation of intention to return: to be sent by employer not earlier than 49 days after the start of the expected week of confinement, or the actual date, whichever the employee notified in the first notification.

Dear Ms X,
This is to ask you whether you still intend to return to work. If you do, I must inform you that you are required to give me confirmation of your intention to return in writing, within 14 days of receiving this letter, unless it is not reasonably practicable for you to do so within that time (in which case you must reply as soon as is reasonably practicable). Failure to reply within this time limit will mean that you will lose your right to return to work with me.
                          Yours sincerely,
                            A N Other

(3)   Employee's reply to employer's request for confirmation of intention to return: to be made within 14 days of receiving the employer's request (or, if it is not reasonably practicable to reply within that time, as soon as is reasonably practicable afterwards).

Dear Mr Other,
This is to let you know that I still intend to return to work.
                          Yours sincerely,
                            Ophelia X

(4)   Employee's final notification: to be sent not later than 21 days before proposed date of return.

Dear Mr Other,
This is to let you know that I will be coming back to work on 7 March.
                          Yours sincerely,
                            Ophelia X

Absence from work

The general practitioner with a small staff may face great difficulty when handling prolonged or frequent absence by an employee. There are several types of absences from work: certificated or uncertificated sick leave; unauthorised absences, including lateness; and authorised absences (apart from holidays, absence for public duties, antenatal care, maternity leave, and for attending a training course). It may seem presumptuous to advise doctors on how to deal with sickness absence among their staff, but we are all familiar with the proverbial cobbler's children's shoes. Members of any profession or occupation may unknowingly forget or neglect to apply their special knowledge and skills to their own circumstances.

It may be helpful to explain the difference between authorised and unauthorised absences. Each employer will decide for himself the grounds on which absence may be authorised. It is important that you lay down clear rules and that your staff are familiar with these. Your staff should know the parameters within which absence is permissible and you should apply these fairly and consistently. For example, different employers will apply different rules to the circumstances when absence may be authorised for a bereavement. Undoubtedly, you will have your views about how much leave is appropriate and in what circumstances it should be allowed and will decide when leave may be authorised for this reason; but it is vital to decide on a policy and apply it consistently.

In any practice the direct and indirect costs of a high level of absence may be considerable; these may include the cost of providing sick pay, paying additional overtime to other staff, employing temporary staff, a reduction in the standards of your services to patients, disruption to working arrangements, and a lowering of morale, together with increased dissatisfaction among staff. Thus it is worth developing and maintaining a procedure to monitor and control absence from work.

Recognising patterns of absence

There has been considerable research into patterns of absence. Some trends have been found and a summary of these may alert you to the types of absences to watch for in your own practice: (*i*) young people tend to take more frequent and shorter periods of sick leave, and older people longer but less frequent periods; (*ii*) unauthorised absence may be common among new employees; established employees will have learnt the standards of your practice and know how to follow these (see "Looking after your new employee"); (*iii*) fortunately for the general practitioner, the incidence of absence from work is a far greater problem in large and impersonal organisations but when it occurs in a small organisation the effects may be disproportionately disruptive.

It is difficult to deal with absenteeism unless you can establish the facts of each case and have kept adequate records. If all absences are recorded you will be in a better position to identify problem areas and also ensure that any action that you take is fair and reasonable. The principle of consistency may be embodied in the procedure (however informal or simple it may be) that you choose to apply when investigating and dealing with any case of frequent or prolonged absence.

Dealing with long term sickness

Absence because of long term illness is almost always a most difficult problem to handle, especially in a small organisation. If one of your staff is away sick for a long time, or is unable to come to work regularly and consistently because of chronic ill health, you are faced with the unwelcome task of keeping the job open to offer security to your sick employee, and thus (it is hoped) help recovery, and having to maintain the standard of service in the surgery. Your predicament is even greater if the sick employee has had long service with you and occupies a key position in the daily running of the surgery. Doctors probably find this dilemma even more intractable than most employers. Not only do they have the good fortune of being blessed with particularly loyal and long serving staff, but their professional calling instils empathy and compassion for chronic ill health.

There is obviously no easy answer to this problem, and the decision that you finally reach will depend on the circumstances of your own practice. It may be helpful, however, to consider the following questions if only to ensure that you have assessed the available options:

(1) Just how much difficulty is being caused by this employee's absence? How long can you manage without a replacement? Can you fill the post satisfactorily temporarily? (Do not forget to ensure that your temporary replacement is aware that the job is temporary.) Can the work be shared or reorganised to accommodate a long term absence? Are your other staff willing to accept an additional workload or responsibility for a prolonged (and possibly indefinite) period?

(2) Have you obtained a prognosis from your employee's general practitioner? The Access to Medical Records Act 1988 now requires employers to notify employees of such an intention and to obtain consent. Such a notification must inform the employee of their rights under the Act, that is, to withhold consent, to have access to the report before it is forwarded to you, and to be able to amend details which they consider incorrect or misleading. Have you considered seeking an independent medical opinion? Is a full recovery likely or will the employee be unlikely ever to return to the old job? (Particular difficulties may arise if one of the partners is the employee's general practitioner. An obvious conflict of interest may arise and may make your decision more difficult to reach. Although as the employee's own general practitioner you should have full knowledge of the prognosis, it may be advisable to obtain an independent medical opinion before you reach a final decision. In circumstances where this is practicable, adjacent practices have been known to agree an informal arrangement whereby staff are encouraged to register in the neighbouring practice even if they were on one of the partner's lists when they originally joined the practice staff. But such an arrangement is not always feasible, especially in rural areas.)

(3) Could your employee return to work if special arrangements were made—for example, could help be given with transport, the work reorganised, or the job redesigned?

(4) Are you likely to have any alternative, lighter, or less stressful work available? Would a part time job be feasible? Could a full time job be shared?

(5) The age and length of service of your sick employee will be vital considerations. Would early retirement be a mutually acceptable solution, perhaps with an enhanced pension or an ex gratia payment?

(6) Can you help the employee to find more suitable employment elsewhere in your locality? A general practitioner may be well placed to give such help.

Whatever conclusion you reach after taking these and any other factors into account, it is most important that your employee is made aware of the position. On medical and humanitarian grounds there may be good reasons for leaving the matter in the air, implying that you will accept the employee back when she has recovered. But this deliberate "indecision" must eventually come to an end when you feel that the job can no longer be kept open. At this stage you must inform the sick employee without delay.

Dealing with short term sickness

There are several steps that may be taken to control the level of sickness absence: (i) your practice manager can have an informal talk with your employee to see if any special help is required; (ii) you may wish to obtain an independent medical opinion on any employee who has frequent sickness absences; (iii) try to ensure that you have a proper procedure on the provision of medical certificates and that all your staff understand and follow this policy—for example, notification of sickness should be made as early as possible on the first day of sickness; (iv) where necessary the employee may need to be told that the level of sick absence is putting the job at risk.

In discussing the statutory sick pay scheme further on I mention the possibilities of operating a system of "self certification" for sickness absence of up to one week. The requirement to give a formal written statement of the reasons for his or her absence can help to concentrate an employee's mind on this important matter.

Frequent absence may indicate general ill health which requires medical investigation and attention, and if it continues it may suggest that the employee is unable to continue to do the job.

Obviously, any general practitioner will encourage his staff to seek medical attention. Furthermore, you may need to explore whether there are any personal or domestic difficulties, or problems with the job itself. Particular attention needs to be paid to any pattern in frequent short absences on grounds of sickness; this may indicate that sickness is being used as a cover for other reasons, and may emphasise the need for good supervision of staff.

Dealing with unauthorised absences, including lateness

Unauthorised absence, the occasional day off work, when sickness is often given as a reason or excuse, is generally known as "absenteeism." Lateness and poor time keeping often reflect the same syndrome. All such absences may be disruptive, particularly because they occur without any prior warning, although ironically enough they may become so patterned that others can predict when they will occur. "She always takes a day off sick before a bank holiday weekend."

Absenteeism and lateness often point to problems arising from the job itself; your employee may be reluctant to come to work because he or she is unhappy in the job, or simply doesn't like work. These problems need to be closely investigated. Is the supervision of your staff adequate? Are working relationships satisfactory? Is the job properly organised in terms of the quantity and quality of the work? Above all, such absenteeism must never be allowed to go unnoticed; you or your practice manager should inquire into the matter without any delay.

Other actions to be taken include: (*i*) keep a careful check of the individual's record of absenteeism, time keeping, etc; (*ii*) insist that the absent employee (or a member of the family or friend) should telephone the surgery before a specified time on the first day of absence (say 11 00 am); (*iii*) obtain some indication of how long the employee is likely to be away, which will help you to cope with the absence; but you may wish to require your employee to ring before a specified time on each day of absence; (*iv*) ensure that the employee has an informal talk with your practice manager on the day immediately after the period of absence; (*v*) watch closely any absences that are next to holidays and look for other obvious patterns; (*vi*) look at the working environment—could this be contributing to absenteeism?

Continued absences of this type may well lead to disciplinary action, which eventually ends in dismissal. The disciplinary procedures that you should follow are outlined next.

Fair, firm, and sympathetic approach

Most general practitioners will rely on their practice managers to deal effectively with absence. He or she will need to be fair, firm, and sympathetic when handling the many varied and often difficult problems that lead to absences from work. To ensure fairness your procedures should be applied with consistency and your employees should be aware of these. To be firm in your approach to absence, you must never hesitate to act if you have good grounds for believing that sickness is being used as an excuse for indefensible absences. Sympathy is particularly necessary when dealing with long term sickness and special domestic or travelling difficulties. Much goodwill may be generated by giving staff authorised time off to meet occasional special needs—for example, the illness of a child or dependent relative, a family bereavement, or specific religious observances of minority groups.

I am most grateful to Dr Ewen Bramwell and Mr Peter Syson and his colleagues of ACAS for their comments on this paper. I am, of course, responsible for any omissions or errors.

Dismissal: fair or unfair?

Mere mention of "dismissal" strikes a note of fear in the hearts of many employers, and general practitioners are no exception. It conjures up a vision of the unpleasant task of sacking an employee and the ensuing risk of defending your action in public at an industrial tribunal. This article seeks to offer reassurance on a vexatious subject.

Questions general practitioners ask

There is no better point to start from than the anxieties often expressed by general practitioners. Firstly, some doctors believe that the plethora of employment law has so tied their hands that it is not only difficult, but virtually impossible, to sack an employee. Secondly, some doctors are so reluctant to contemplate dismissal, even when this is clearly necessary that they compound their problems by delay and a failure to follow a proper procedure. Indeed, some doctors are so reticent that they are unwilling to dismiss a newly recruited employee who (even after adequate training and supervision) is quite unsuited to the job. Reluctance to dismiss may be associated with a failure to give proper notice of the dismissal and to follow the required procedure. These omissions almost always create greater difficulties and may so easily lead to a successful claim for compensation for unfair dismissal. Other problems arise if doctors try to use redundancy as the grounds for dismissal when the actual reasons are to do with misconduct or inability to do the job.

Sometimes a general practitioner fails to consult his partners before taking action even though the decision should be taken (or at the very least confirmed) by the partnership as a whole. A more unusual (almost bizarre) problem occurs when a general practitioner tries to dismiss someone who is not even his employee; the most common example is an attempted dismissal of a health authority employee attached to a practice.

The content and quantity of work is always changing; your employees change through normal wastage, and their own domestic circumstances, health, and capabilities will also alter. More generally, there will be changes in the way in which a practice is run; practices may combine or divide, premises may be acquired or closed, and new work may be taken on. All these changes may lead to a position where an employee is either unwilling to do the work that is required or incapable of doing it.

The need for change and for your employees to accept and adapt to it inevitably creates many "grey areas" which do not seem to fit easily into the formalities of the unfair dismissal legislation. Other articles discuss ways of handling this continual process of change and adaptation, in particular those on "How to change a contract of employment" and "Absence from work." The crucial guiding principle is that you should ensure that your staff are aware that change is an inevitable feature of your practice and that they should be willing to accept this and be capable of adapting to it. If they fall short in either of these respects then the procedures outlined below may have to be applied.

What is dismissal?

In most circumstances it is clear to both the employee and the employer when a dismissal takes place. But note that a dismissal may also occur when: (a) An employee's fixed term contract expires and is not renewed. (It is not normally advisable to work with fixed term contracts, particularly if these are extended on a year by year basis.) (b) An employer does not allow an employee who has qualified for reinstatement to return to work after pregnancy. (c) An employee resigns for reasons that relate to certain conduct by the employer—this is known as "constructive dismissal". (d) An employer does not make his intentions clear—for example, if his language or expression is unclear. Although a dismissal may not be intended, certain phrases—such as, "You know what you can do"—in fact may reasonably be interpreted as notice of dismissal.

Fair reasons for dismissal

There are several aspects to any dismissal that determine whether it is fair or unfair: (*a*) Is the reason for the dismissal valid? (*b*) Has the employer acted reasonably in treating that reason as sufficient grounds for dismissing the employee? (*c*) Is the procedure followed by the employer fair?

The legislation refers to five specific types of reason that may justify dismissal.

Conduct—That is the most usual reason for dismissal and the one that is most likely to lead to a complaint of unfair dismissal.

Capability—The employee cannot satisfactorily do the job. Additional problems that may arise when illness has led to an employee being unable to do the job are discussed below.

Redundancy—Normally an employee has no grounds for claiming unfair dismissal if the dismissal was because of redundancy—that is, because the employer has no work (or insufficient work) for the employee to do and is unable to provide suitable alternative work. It is not uncommon, however, for redundancy to be used improperly as an easier alternative to "misconduct" or "incapacity" to effect a dismissal.

A statutory requirement—The most obvious example is when the loss of a driving licence prevents an employee from doing the job and there is no suitable alternative job available.

Some other substantial reason—This may sound like a Catch 22 option, but in fact it applies to the specific and important range of circumstances described below.

Grounds for dismissal

Misconduct

If you dismiss a member of your staff on the grounds of misconduct this will usually be the final stage of your disciplinary procedure. When contemplating or taking this action you need to consider the following:

(1) Did your employee know an offence was being committed? Your disciplinary rules should be sensible and clear and your staff should be aware of them. It is essential that they should know of any conduct which constitutes gross misconduct because this could result in suspension from work on full pay, pending an

investigation that may precede summary dismissal—that is, without notice. Obviously, anything you label as gross misconduct must be serious enough to warrant summary dismissal. For general practitioners' staff a serious breach of confidentiality, an act of theft, or an abuse of drugs are examples of gross misconduct. It is advisable to give examples of these in your written contract of employment.

(2) It is quite unreasonable for someone to be dismissed for a first offence, except where there has been gross misconduct. If you are considering dismissal your employee should have been warned on a previous occasion when misconduct occurred that further offences might lead to dismissal. It is advisable to give written warnings to an employee in line with the ACAS code which is mentioned below. These may have an impact, particularly if it is made clear that it is a final written warning and that a further repetition will lead to dismissal. You may wish to ask your employee to confirm in writing her receipt of your letter. It is certainly advisable to keep a written record of all your warnings not only for your own use but also as evidence if you should be faced with an industrial tribunal hearing. [It is normal for written warnings to be kept "on record" for only a specified period—say, for 12 months.]

(3) You must investigate all the facts of the case thoroughly, particularly if it is likely to lead to a summary dismissal.

(4) Finally, if your procedures are reasonable your employees should have an opportunity to put their side of the case. There might be an acceptable explanation for the behaviour.

The Advisory, Conciliation and Arbitration Service (ACAS) have produced a code on disciplinary practice and procedures, and industrial tribunals have to take this into account when deciding whether a dismissal was fair or unfair. It is recognised that the small employer cannot be expected to follow this code to the letter. If your approach to a dismissal takes account of the issues discussed above, the main points of the ACAS code will have been covered.

Inability to do the job

There are various grounds on which an employee might be considered unable to do the job—ill health, lack of skill or qualifications, poor standard of performance.

Before you contemplate dismissing an employee on grounds of inability you should consider the following: (*a*) Have you provided adequate training including guidance on how the work should be done and the standards you expect? (*b*) Has your employee been properly supervised? Have you provided regular opportunities to discuss and review progress? (*c*) Has your employee been told of any shortcomings as soon as these became evident? Has there been an opportunity to improve? (It is important not to allow matters to drift on.) (*d*) Is the employee in the right job? If not, within the limited opportunities available could the employee be offered something more suitable? (*e*) Have you given a final warning, stating that if there is no improvement the employee will be dismissed?

More difficult problems arise when employees are absent through ill health (see "Absence from work"). An employer with few employees may find it hard to cope with frequent or prolonged absences. The employer may be unable to keep the job open indefinitely.

Redundancy

Fortunately, redundancy is a rare occurrence in general practice, although it has been known to happen. Although it may be fair to dismiss an employee on these grounds because you need fewer people to do your work, you must be in a position to show that your method of selecting who should go was fair. This is vital. You should decide on the criteria of selection—for example, length of service, skill, an objective assessment of work performance, attendance, disciplinary warnings, or some combination of these, you should then consider whether there is any other job available for the person who is being made redundant; and finally you should try to give as much warning as possible.

Legal impediments to continued employment

An employee may be fairly dismissed if continued employment would result in a breach of the law. The obvious example is when someone who is employed to drive loses his or her licence. Nevertheless, even though this case may seem straightforward, it is still necessary for you to be able to show that you have acted

DISMISSAL: FAIR OR UNFAIR?

reasonably. In particular, you would need to consider whether driving was essential to the job and whether alternative work would be available, albeit on a short term basis until the licence is restored.

Other substantial reasons

There are other grounds that justify dismissal not covered by the headings above. It is difficult to specify these with precision but industrial tribunals have accepted the following as "some other substantial reason" for fair dismissal: (*i*) difficult relationships with other staff; (*ii*) changes of duties or conditions that were not acceptable to the employee (see "How to change a contract of employment"); (*iii*) false information (which has importance) on an application form; (*iv*) reorganisation of a business; (*v*) when a temporary replacement for another employee—for example, during maternity leave—is no longer required.

In all these circumstances you should ensure that the dismissal is carried out in a reasonable manner, giving a proper explanation and due warning. Your reasons for the dismissal should be put in writing, and you should make some provision in your disciplinary procedure for your employee to appeal against your decision.

Who may not complain of unfair dismissal?

The main circumstances where someone cannot complain of unfair dismissal are:

(1) Anyone who is not an employee—for example, an independent contractor. There have been recent industrial tribunal cases where a general practitioner has been able to lodge a claim for unfair dismissal (following the termination of a partnership) because the contractual agreement between the partners did not meet the criteria of a partnership as defined in the law of partnership. In such circumstances the consequences may be more far reaching and serious than just the risk of a successful claim for compensation on the grounds of unfair dismissal.

(2) Employees who have not completed two years' continuous employment by the date on which dismissal takes place.

(3) Employees who normally work fewer than 16 hours a week,

unless they have been employed continuously for at least eight hours a week for at least five years.

(4) Employees who have already reached the normal retiring age for their employment or, if there is no normal retiring age, both men and women who have reached age 65.

Unfair dismissal in perspective

It should be the aim of any employer to act in a fair and reasonable way in all his dealings with staff. This is in the interests of good management, and employment legislation is designed to encourage and support it.

Note these three features of the legislation:

(1) An employee cannot normally bring an unfair dismissal claim to an industrial tribunal until she has been with you for two years.

(2) Industrial tribunals must take into account the size and administrative resources of the employer when considering whether a dismissal is fair to reduce the burden on small employers.

(3) Although rare in general practice, any dismissal based on discrimination against trade union activities, or concerning action against anyone who has made a claim of sexual or racial discrimination, will be judged automatically unfair.

Some recent statistics offer reassurance. Less than a tenth of all dismissals in any year lead to unfair dismissal claims, only 3% of all dismissals actually lead to a tribunal hearing, and less than 1% are found to be unfair. Some two thirds of unfair dismissal claims are settled before any tribunal hearings, many are withdrawn, and the rest are settled by agreed compensation, often by using the services of an independent ACAS conciliation officer.

Where cases went forward to a tribunal hearing, in only about a quarter of these was the dismissal found to be unfair. Some recent statistics show that the amount of compensation awarded by tribunals was less than £750 in about one third of the unfair "cases," less than £1500 in over half of them. In only 4% of cases was the award over £6000.

Although these figures are reassuring, a tribunal hearing may be a harrowing experience and the work required to prepare your defence and attend the hearings is both costly and time consuming to you and the practice. Thus it is advisable to take some simple precautionary steps, particularly since these may also help you to manage your practice more effectively.

Preventive measures

Dismissal should be a rare event if you have already followed the steps below, which have been described in the chapters on "how to change a contract of employment," "recruiting surgery staff," and "employment law."

(1) Make sure that your selection procedures are adequate so that you find the right person to fill your vacancy. Ensure that your practice manager fully participates in selecting a new member of staff.

(2) Relations with a new employee should be put on a proper footing from the outset. You are legally obliged to issue a written statement of the main terms and conditions of their employment within 13 weeks of the employee starting work in your practice. This statement should specify any disciplinary rules (or refer to another document containing these) and state to whom the employee should go if she is dissatisfied with any disciplinary decision affecting her, or if she has a grievance about the job. The importance of having adequate disciplinary and grievance procedures has been emphasised in the chapter on "employment law."

(3) Try to ensure that your training arrangements are satisfactory. It is important to act without delay if the standard of work falls below what you require. Difficult and almost intractable problems may arise if you allow unsatisfactory working practices to persist simply because you are reluctant to take corrective action. Your employee will assume acceptance of unsatisfactory performance if no action is required to improve it.

(4) Written records are most important. You should keep notes of any disciplinary warnings (oral or written warnings) since these may be required as evidence if your actions ultimately lead to dismissal and a subsequent tribunal hearing.

If these steps are followed you are unlikely to face problems over dismissal. Nevertheless, even the most conscientious employer may have to consider a dismissal. Should this happen it cannot be emphasised too often that *there is normally a two year qualifying period before a claim of unfair dismissal may be made.* This should provide ample time for you to assess someone's capabilities. A new employee will serve a specified probationary period, but you have up to two years to monitor performance before statutory rights are acquired. Your employee should be given the chance to improve before and after the two year qualifying period.

Reassurance

As I have stated above, unfair dismissal is a rare occurrence. Indeed, when it does happen it is often a consequence of an ill considered approach to the necessary disciplinary action that must precede dismissal. This in turn usually arises from the general practitioner's reluctance to act decisively (but reasonably) when this is necessary. Indeed, it has been the doctor's own kindness and unwillingness to upset one of his staff which has subsequently led to serious legal difficulties and even a tribunal hearing. Preventive action is crucial, not only because it is a necessary part of good management, but also because it will avoid the trauma of a claim of unfair dismissal.

Remember that your handling of any dismissal has both "procedural" and "substantive" aspects. It is necessary to show that your approach to it has been fair and reasonable and that the reasons for the dismissal are reasonable, and therefore defensible, if you should be required to justify your actions.

Lastly, if you have the misfortune of being the subject of an industrial tribunal application (and hearing) you should seek advice from your local BMA regional office without delay. Whether you win or lose the case, it is advisable to consider whether any lessons may be learnt from the episode. Was your selection procedure lacking in some respect? Is your disciplinary procedure effective, especially your arrangements to give an early warning of unsatisfactory performance or behaviour?

I am most grateful to Dr John Ball, Dr Ewen Bramwell, and Mr Peter Syson and his colleagues of ACAS for their comments on this paper. I am, of course, responsible for any omissions or errors.

Discrimination in employment

Few general practitioners will have experienced any difficulties with the race and sex discrimination laws. Indeed, for any employer, avoiding discrimination per se is good management. It may seem unlikely that an employer with only a handful of staff (most of whom are already women) could be affected in any way. Both the Race Relations Act and the Sex Discrimination Act apply to any employer, irrespective of the size of his undertaking. Previously the Sex Discrimination Act applied to all employers apart from those with five employees or fewer; the government introduced legislation which removed this exemption for the small employer.

There is a growing awareness among the public of these anti-discrimination laws. This has been heightened by the present economic climate and the efforts of various organisations (including local councils and voluntary agencies) to inform people of their rights and to encourage and assist them in pursuing these. Various public bodies, including the Commission for Racial Equality, the Equal Opportunities Commission, and local community relations councils have been particularly active in this sphere. It is therefore more likely than before that an unsuccessful applicant to a vacancy in your practice (or someone unknown to you who has not even applied for the vacancy) could seek redress on the grounds that your recruitment and selection procedures were discriminatory.

Fortunately, the small employer can greatly reduce any risk of an unjustifiable claim of discrimination by taking a few essential precautionary steps. Any claim of discrimination incurs the time and costs of attending an industrial tribunal hearing. If successful, there are the additional costs of the compensatory award. Irrespective of its outcome the claim may lead to unwelcome local publicity.

Extent of anti-discrimination law

There are two areas where legislation requires an employer to act (and to be able to show that he has acted) in a manner that is not discriminatory: (*i*) on the grounds of sex (including equal pay) and marital status; (*ii*) on the grounds of colour, race, nationality (including citizenship), or ethnic or national origins.

If your recruitment and selection procedures, together with your employment practices, are properly conducted no difficulties should ever arise. The sex discrimination legislation was primarily intended to raise the opportunities and status of women in employment; however, men do have equal rights under this Act.

Fortunately, the scope and structure of both the sex and racial discrimination law are similar. Both include two types of discrimination, direct and indirect, and both require employers to take essentially the same action to ensure that their behaviour is neither discriminatory in practice nor capable of being seen as such.

Direct discrimination occurs when a person treats another person less favourably on grounds of race (or sex, or both) than he treats (or would treat) someone else. It is not necessary to show that the person openly expressed an intention to discriminate; it is possible in many instances to infer that his motive was discriminatory in the light of the circumstances of his actions.

Indirect discrimination occurs when the treatment may be equal in a formal sense as between different racial groups or between persons of different sex, but is discriminatory in its effect on one sex or particular racial group—for example, the unnecessary stipulation that a cleaner should have certain educational qualifications.

When assessing whether or not an employer has acted in an indirectly discriminatory manner an industrial tribunal is required to consider whether his actions, although formally applied in a non-discriminatory manner, have the effect of being discriminatory. In the area of racial discrimination, indirect discrimination would have occurred in filling a vacancy if the following consequences occurred. The employer imposed some condition which any applicant for his vacancy must fulfil. Although this condition is applied equally to everyone irrespective of racial group, its effect is to debar persons of a particular racial group from either applying or successfully competing for the job. In these circumstances his action may provide a basis for a claim of indirect discrimination. In particular, the tribunal will consider whether the proportion of persons able to satisfy the condition in the "complainant's" racial group is considerably smaller than the proportion outside that group who can comply with it. If it can then be shown that the condition cannot be justified in terms of what is required for the job, indirect racial discrimination will have occurred. A similar approach is applied when assessing whether any employer's behaviour is indirectly discriminatory on grounds of sex.

There are three areas where it is unlawful to discriminate on grounds of race or sex when recruiting staff: *(a)* In the arrangements you make for deciding who should be offered the job—for example, in the instructions you give to an employment agency or in the way in which the job is advertised. (In practice an employment agency or newspaper should ensure that your vacancy is neither advertised nor handled in a way which is discriminatory on grounds of race or sex.) The person claiming that he or she has been discriminated against does not need to have applied for the job to be eligible to make a complaint about these arrangements. *(b)* In relation to any terms offered—for example, pay or holidays. *(c)* By refusing or deliberately omitting to offer a person employment—for example, by rejecting an application or by deliberately avoiding consideration of an application.

It is also unlawful for an employer to discriminate on grounds of sex or race in the opportunities he provides for his employees for promotion or training, or any other benefits, facilities, or services. It is especially important to ensure that your procedures for promotion are fair, since this is where discrimination can most easily creep in.

(Although not related to employment as such, it should be noted that it is unlawful for any partnership to discriminate on grounds of race or sex in the arrangements it makes for the selection of new partners, in affording a partner access to benefits, facilities, or services, in opportunities for training, in dismissing a partner, or in treating the partner unfavourably in any other way. These provisions also apply to persons proposing to form themselves into a partnership.)

No discrimination against part time employees: a possible future EC directive

The European Commission has been considering a draft directive to prevent discrimination against part time staff, and the United Kingdom is considering its response to these proposals. In general, it is considered to be a matter of good employment practice to treat part time staff on an equal footing to full time staff. The aim of this directive would be to improve the employment opportunities and status of women; in particular it would assist the transition of part time work and the return to full time work of women with domestic commitments.

The specific aims of the draft directive are: (*i*) to ensure that the principle of non-discrimination as between part time and full time staff is universally implemented; (*ii*) to provide for part time employees to receive proportional rights in respect of pay, holiday pay, and pensions; (*iii*) to provide that part time employees should be given a written statement of their terms and conditions of employment; (*iv*) to give priority within an undertaking to part time staff if they wish to transfer to full time employment (and vice versa).

It will take some time for these proposals to be fully considered in Europe and even longer before they are adopted by all member states.

Points to watch

The most important matter on which you may need to concentrate is the arrangements you make for selecting and recruiting staff. The more informal your methods the greater the risk of being accused of discrimination, particularly on grounds of race. An approach to recruitment based on an informal by "word of mouth" method may not only have unforeseen dangers of its own (see "recruiting ancillary staff"), but it can easily leave you open to a claim (even for someone unknown to you who has not even applied for the vacancy) that your selection procedure is discriminatory. It is wise to retain the notes you make at the time of the interview.

The current level of unemployment, together with changes of attitudes, may lead to more men applying for receptionist and secretarial posts, work which has been seen as a traditional preserve of women. Applications from men need to be considered on the same basis as those for women.

There are genuine occupational qualifications that allow some jobs to be excluded from the sex discrimination law. But it is most unlikely that many (if any) posts in general practice would satisfy these. The Sex Discrimination Act removed the legal barriers to men becoming midwives.

Any individual who considers that he or she is a victim of discriminatory action may institute proceedings in an industrial tribunal if the action complained of is in the employment field. Few problems are likely to arise for general practitioners, but there is growing public awareness of this legislation. The sex and race discrimination laws are intended to encourage and reinforce good employment practices. It is these good practices that are important, and this legislation should not be approached from the standpoint of how to meet its basic statutory requirements.

Further information may be obtained from the following:

On sex discrimin ion: Equal Opportunities Commission, Overseas House, Quay Street, Manchester M3 3HN, Tel: 061–833 9244.

On race discrimination: Commission for Racial Equality, Elliot House, 10–12 Allington Street, London SW1E 5EH, Tel: 01–828 7022.

I am grateful to Dr Ewen Bramwell and Mr Peter Syson and his colleagues of ACAS for their comments on this paper. I am, of course, responsible for any omissions or errors.

Hiring part time staff

Many general practitioners employ part time ancillary staff. When a full time post becomes vacant there may be a choice between finding a full time replacement, employing two or more part time staff, or not filling the vacancy. Most general practitioners undoubtedly choose between these options intuitively. The choice probably depends on the availability of suitable staff, on whether existing full time staff are willing to work longer hours, or simply on the traditions of their practice organisation. Only the general practitioner and his or her partners can decide which staffing arrangements are best suited to their particular needs. Some factors that may need to be taken into account when reaching a decision are the costs and benefits of employing either whole time or part time employees, and the legal, financial, and administrative implications of these employment arrangements.

Advantages and disadvantages

Some advantages of employing part time staff are:

(1) Staffing levels can be matched more easily with predictable levels of work load. Part timers can provide additional cover during busy periods and allow staffing levels to be cut during slack periods, thus reducing total staff costs.

(2) Most surgery staff are often reluctant to take sick leave. But there is reputedly a lower rate of absenteeism among part time staff; domestic commitments and appointments can be arranged during the employee's own time.

(3) The use of part time staff can reduce the need for additional payments to full time staff for overtime or unsocial hours.

(4) The surgery may be more easily run continuously with part

time staff by providing cover for meal breaks and the early morning and evening shifts.

(5) There is a comparatively new option of job sharing, which is growing in popularity. This arrangement enables two people to agree to share the responsibilities of a single full time job and the pay and benefits in proportion to the hours each works.

Disadvantages of employing part time staff may include:

(1) Problems of continuity may still arise if there is difficulty in matching morning, afternoon, and evening shifts.

(2) The purely administrative costs of employing two part timers are often higher than those of one full time employee.

(3) The rate of turnover—that is, resignation—among part timers is often higher; their commitment to the employer may be weaker, and their earnings may not be so important in relation to the total family income.

(4) They may be less committed to the practice than full time staff and thus may be less willing to acquire new skills and to be flexible in their working arrangements.

Employment rights of part time staff

In general the part time employee has fewer rights of employment protection than his or her full time counterpart. But the law is precise about who is a part time employee for the purposes of employment protection rights and which rights apply to all employees, irrespective of how many hours a week they work.

The law regards all employees who work 16 or more hours a week and employees who work between eight and 16 hours a week and also have five years' continuous service as qualifying for certain employment rights. Those employment rights which are dependent on the number of hours worked are listed in the table.

Employees working less than eight hours a week have no claim to any of these employment rights. But certain other employment rights apply universally and are not dependent on the number of hours worked or length of service. These include rights under the Equal Pay, Sex Discrimination, and Race Relations Acts; victimisation or discrimination for trade union activities; and rights to paid time off for antenatal care.

Employment right	Length of service required for employees working 16 + hours a week
Redundancy pay	2 years after age 18
Statutory maternity pay	26 weeks before 15th week before expected date of confinement
Unfair dismissal	2 years
Written reasons for dismissal	6 months*
Written particulars of employment	Immediately (the employer has 13 weeks in which to supply it)
Minimum notice	1 month
Guaranteed pay	1 month
Dismissal connected with medical suspension	1 month
Time off for trade union duties, training, activities, and public duties; and itemised pay statement	None

* Will increase to two years when the current Employment Bill is enacted during 1989.

What happens if the hours of work are changed?

If an employee is employed initially under a contract of 16 hours or more a week, but his or her hours are subsequently temporarily reduced to under 16 (but remain more than eight hours a week) each week of working this reduced week will still count towards length of service requirements, up to a maximum period of 26 weeks.

In addition, when a particular employment right requires a minimum period of continuous service and the employee has already qualified for it, if the employee's contracted hours are subsequently reduced to between eight and 16 hours a week he or she will not lose the rights already acquired.

Variable patterns of part time working

The number of hours worked by part timers can vary from week to week. Some may be working by arrangement alternate weeks— that is, full time working one week and the following week off. Under this arrangement staff are often considered to be continuously in employment during the week off and therefore they do not lose their employment rights.

Administering part time contracts

If the part time employee has more than one part time job income tax may be deducted by either the principal employer or by two or more employers. The tax office will make the necessary arrangements by allotting an appropriate coding.

For National Insurance, the lower earnings limit is currently £43, and this is reviewed annually. If an employee earns less than £43 a week neither the employer nor the employee pays National Insurance contributions on the employee's earnings. If, however, the employee earns an amount greater than or equal to this both employer and employee pay contributions on the whole of the employee's earnings. Savings may be made if a pattern of hours is agreed so that total pay does not exceed the lower earnings limit.

Married women who are part time employees (and full time employees) earning £43 or more may be paying either full rate class 1 National Insurance contributions or the lower rate married women's contributions. But since May 1977 the option of paying a married women's rate of contribution has been phased out. Married women who paid the lower rate before May 1977 may continue to do so. If a married woman has been away from employment for two complete tax years she must pay the full rate of contribution when she returns to work.

Hours of work and pay

The hours of work of part time staff vary greatly according to the needs of the practice. Some part timers may be employed two or three hours a day to cover the midday meal break or the busy periods during morning, afternoon, or evening surgery. Other arrangements may require only a couple of hours a day two or three days a week, or even a few hours on alternate weeks.

It is not uncommon to find that part time employees are paid at a lower hourly rate than full timers. If the part time employees are women (over 95% of part time staff are women) it may appear that they could claim that they were being discriminated against under the Equal Pay Act. The provisions of this Act, however, now require a woman to compare her position with a man doing similar work, but the government is reviewing this requirement after a recent judgment of the Court of Justice of the European Community. Since it is unlikely that a man will be doing similar work to a part time woman employee there are rarely any grounds for a case to be brought. Thus, if all your part time staff are women there is

81

no legislation to prevent you from paying a different hourly rate from that paid to full time staff. But this may be affected by the European Commission "directive" mentioned below.

Should part time staff be paid overtime rates? There are different views of what constitutes "overtime" for such staff: (*i*) any work in excess of a full time working week—for example, beyond 40 hours a week; (*ii*) any work in excess of daily full time hours—for example, beyond eight hours a day; (*iii*) any work after normal business hours—for example, working well beyond the end of evening surgery; (*iv*) any work in excess of the contracted part time hours.

In practice most employers pay overtime rates to part timers only when they work beyond the full time working week. And this will in turn depend on whether any full time staff are paid overtime rates. The danger of paying part timers overtime rates for time worked in excess of their part time hours is that your full time staff may see it as being unfair to them, and they may prefer to opt for part time contracts so that they benefit from these premium rates. One arrangement may be to decide to fix the part time rate as a percentage of the full time rate—say, 80%—and then to pay an overtime premium rate to part time staff, which brings them into line with the basic full time hourly rate.

Pension arrangements

Part time staff rarely qualify for occupational pension schemes. Their entitlement to state basic pensions depends on their record of National Insurance contributions. A married woman over the age of 60 can only qualify in her own right if she has paid full rate National Insurance contributions for a qualifying period. If she has opted for the married woman's reduced rate of National Insurance contribution she only qualifies for the lower rate of pension on her husband's contributions.

Maternity arrangements

A pregnant employee may acquire these statutory legal rights: (*i*) to return to work with her employer after maternity leave; (*ii*) to receive statutory maternity pay; (*iii*) to complain of unfair dismissal if her employer dismisses her because of pregnancy; (*iv*) not to be "unreasonably" refused paid time off for antenatal care.

A minimum period of service must be completed for the first three of these rights, but not for the fourth.

Maternity leave

A woman employee is entitled to take up to a maximum of 40 weeks' maternity leave (starting any time after the 11th week before the baby is due, together with 29 weeks after the birth). The period of leave may be extended in certain circumstances. Entitlement to maternity leave depends on the employee having 104 weeks' continuous service if she works 16 or more hours a week. This period of service must be fulfilled before the 11th week before the expected date of confinement. If the woman works between eight and 16 hours a week and has had five years' continuous service before the 11th week before the expected date of confinement she also qualifies for the 40 week maximum statutory period of maternity leave. Women who work less than eight hours a week have no legal rights to maternity leave.

Any woman who qualifies for maternity leave is also entitled to return either to her previous job or to other suitable work if it is not "reasonably practicable" for her employer to offer her previous job back. But, if the employer has five or fewer employees the woman cannot claim unfair dismissal if he finds it impracticable to take her back. After her maternity leave a woman may prefer to return to work part time. There is no statutory legal obligation on an employer to agree to this arrangement, and it may be particularly difficult for an employer with few staff to adjust his staffing to accommodate this change.

Statutory maternity pay

The qualifying conditions for statutory maternity pay (SMP) are different from those for maternity leave. These are explained in detail on pages 52 to 54. Part time staff are eligible to be paid SMP if they have 26 weeks' continuous employment, normally weekly earnings of not less than the National Insurance (NI) lower limit and give 21 days' prior notice of intended absence. Employees with two years' continuous employment working for 16 hours a week or more are eligible for a higher SMP rate for the first six weeks.

Unfair dismissal

It is automatically unfair to dismiss an employee because she is pregnant if she has qualified by length of service to complain of unfair dismissal. There are certain specific exceptions to this general principle.

Paid time off for antenatal care

All pregnant employees have a right to take "reasonable" paid time off to attend antenatal clinics. Except for a request for a first appointment, the employee may be asked by her employer to produce a certificate stating that she is pregnant and an appointment card showing the time of her appointment. Because this is a comparatively new statutory legal right few problems have arisen. It may be reasonable, however, for an employer to ask a part time employee to try to arrange the appointment outside working hours.

Holiday pay and sick pay

Current employment legislation does not require any employer to pay an employee during holiday periods. Moreover, if you provide holiday pay for full time employees, there is no obligation to extend these arrangements to cover part time employees. The same discretion also applies to the arrangements you may wish to make for public holidays. But it is advisable to let your employees know in advance which arrangement you intend to apply.

The right to receive statutory sick pay depends on an employee's National Insurance contributions. To qualify, an employee must have paid class 1 contributions. Married women who have opted for the reduced National Insurance contributions do not qualify for sickness benefit, though they are eligible for industrial injury benefit.

Since April 1983 part time employees are entitled to receive statutory sick pay from their employers. They qualify for sick pay irrespective of whether they pay the full or reduced National Insurance contributions. The employer is responsible for paying statutory sick pay for the first 28 weeks of an employee's sick leave in a tax year. After this part time employees still on sick leave will only qualify for state sick benefit if they have paid the full rate of National Insurance contributions for the qualifying period. The employer is responsible for keeping certain records. (See DHSS leaflet *Employers Guide to Statutory Sick Pay*, NI 227, October 1985, 43 pages.)

Future legislation

The European Commission is considering a new "directive" that will prevent discrimination against part time employees in their terms of service and to guarantee that they are paid in proportion to full time employees doing equivalent work. The timetable of this legislation is still uncertain; when it is approved by all member countries each will be required to introduce legislation to implement it. Only the UK opposes its introduction.

If this "directive" is implemented it will fundamentally change the status of the part time employee. It sets out to ensure that there is no discrimination as between part time and full time employees and that they enjoy proportional rights with regard to remuneration, holiday pay, redundancy pay, and pensions, that each part timer is provided with a written contract of employment, and that priority is given to employees who seek to transfer from part time to full time employment or vice versa.

Employees should know where they stand

In deciding what arrangements to make for your part time staff you need to make sure that all of your staff know exactly where they stand. The arrangements applying to part timers—that is, their pay, holidays, sick leave, and hours of work—should be spelt out in a written statement of their conditions of service or in a contract of employment. In an earlier chapter on "employment law" a detailed explanation is given of how to prepare a contract. This is only a general guide to the provisions of existing legislation. It does not offer a definitive statement of law.

I am grateful to Dr John Ball for his comments on this paper. I am responsible for any omissions or errors.

Health and Safety at Work Act 1974

For some time general practitioners could assume that legislation on health and safety at work simply need not worry them. But some general practitioners have been surprised by a visit to their premises by a health and safety inspector. The obligations laid down on the employer by the Health and Safety at Work Act etc are not onerous. Most general practitioners undoubtedly occupy premises that meet with the requirements of the legislation, and apart from a few mostly technical matters there is little in this new legislation that should cause concern. Nevertheless, it may be helpful to explain the responsibilities laid on the employer, if only to forewarn general practitioners of some matters that an inspector may raise.

The 1974 Health and Safety at Work Act is not just another Factory Act. It lays down a new approach to occupational health, safety, and welfare, and it applies to many premises that are not covered by previous legislation, including laboratories, hospitals, and general practice surgeries. Although the occupiers of these premises already owed their visitors the "common duty of care," as laid down in the 1957 Occupier's Liability Act, this duty only required reasonable precautions to be taken for their wellbeing and was far less onerous than the duties of many employers to their employees as specified in Factory Acts, the Offices, Shops and Railway Premises Act, and the Mines and Quarries Acts.

The new Health and Safety Executive, combining the factory inspectorate and other central government inspectorate, is responsible to the Health and Safety Commission. Local authority environmental health officers inspect premises and enforce the legislation in the non-industrial sector, and they follow guidance from the Commission. Because general practitioners' premises are grouped with hospitals and laboratories in the category of "health services" it is the Health and Safety Executive that inspects their premises.

The Act lays down new duties on employers (including the self employed) to provide and maintain a safe place of work. It establishes new powers and penalties to enforce safety laws, and its aim is to make all employers and employees aware of the need for safety at the place of work. Although much of this legislation is concerned with employers who already recognise trade unions—there is a requirement to appoint union safety representatives and establish a safety committee if requested to do so—even general practitioners who have only a few employees and do not recognise trade unions have duties to fulfil.

General practitioner's duties to his staff

The most important duties laid down in the Act are those of an employer to an employee. (The general practitioners with ancillary staff who are employed by a health authority have other lesser duties.) The Act states: "It shall be the duty of every employer to ensure, so far as is reasonably practicable, the health, safety, and welfare at work of all his employees." Thus the general practitioner is required to do all that is *reasonably practical* to ensure the safety of his employees. Any proceedings that may be taken under the Act are criminal. An employee can report a breach of the employer's statutory duty under the Act to the Health and Safety Executive, who may bring criminal charges. Although the Act does not in itself confer a right of civil action on the employee, it does not prevent the employee, if injured, suing the employer for being in breach of his liability as an employer or for negligence under the common law.

What is reasonably practicable?

In assessing whether it was reasonably practicable for a general practitioner to avoid a specific hazard or risk of injury a court may well look at the cost of any preventive measures, particularly if the general practitioner's resources are limited, and weigh this against the risk of personal injury and its likely severity. Thus, a larger practice may have a heavier burden imposed than one with few resources.

The Act requires that all equipment and systems of work must be safe and without risk to health. This includes waste bins, sterilisers, photocopying machines, electric fires, electric type-writers, furniture, fire extinguishers, plugs, and any other potentially hazardous equipment. Importance is attached to the maintenance and renewal of equipment, and inspectors are particularly concerned about the arrangements for regular servicing. Attention is also paid to the age, reliability, appropriateness, and position of equipment.

Safe systems of working must be understood and used by all persons. Obvious examples include ensuring that staff do not lift heavy weights without help if there is a risk of back injury, that arrangements are made for the safe disposal of clinical waste, and that care is taken in storing flammable liquids, materials (such as paper), and drugs.

Any offences under the Medicines Act, the Poisons Acts, or the Misuse of Drugs Act 1971, lie outside the remit of the Health and Safety at Work Act. So any unauthorised access to drugs is more likely to be of interest to the Home Office than the Health and Safety Executive.

Misuse of drugs

Since there may be some overlap of the work of these government bodies, brief reference should be made to the Misuse of Drugs Act 1971 and its regulations. Most general practitioners can expect to encounter drug abuse in one form or another. This Act aims at restricting the availability of certain specified drugs of dependence. The following safety precautions apply to such drugs. They must be kept in a "locked receptacle" which can be opened only by the practitioner or a person authorised by him. This does not mean that your duties are absolved if you simply hide the key of this receptacle in a drawer or some other "secret place," since this could be the first place where an unauthorised person might search. Also, the courts do not accept a locked car as a "locked receptacle" within the meaning of the regulations, so emergency bags, if they have to be left in cars, should also be locked.

In large dispensing practices, where substantial quantities of controlled drugs may be stored, the advice of the local crime prevention officer on appropriate security precautions should be obtained. Both the police and inspectors of the Home Office Drugs Branch are concerned with the enforcement of the Misuse of Drugs Act, and any breach is a criminal offence. Further information is available in a booklet *Doctors and the Misuse of Drugs Act, 1971* from the Home Office, 50 Queen Anne's Gate, London SW1.

Written statement of safety policy is required

The general practitioner should provide information, training, and supervision to ensure the health and safety of his ancillary staff. Specifically, unless he employs fewer than five ancillary staff he must prepare a written statement of his general policy "with respect to the health and safety" of his employees and the organisation and arrangements for carrying out this policy. For example, any safety rules that apply to potentially hazardous operations undertaken by medical and nursing staff—the dangers of homologous serum jaundice and "High Risk Specimen" warning stickers required under the Howie Code of Practice for the Prevention of Infection in Clinical Laboratories and Post-Mortem Rooms by all Pathological Laboratories and the immediate action required by staff in respect of accidents and mishaps that might occur. He should consult his employees about its form and content. Although it is not necessary in a small practice to give everybody a copy of this written statement it may be advisable to do so. A group practice may easily overlook a change in their legal obligation when the number of employees increases. The statement could be pinned on a notice board, but if the general practitioner wished to show that it had been drawn to everyone's attention it is advisable to give everyone a copy. Once the requirement to provide a written statement is established—that is, you have five or more employees—it should cover all persons working on the premises.

The statement should be simple and avoid excessive wording that may detract from its impact. But the safety rules should be as comprehensive as necessary so that both the general practitioner and the safety inspector can ensure that the procedures are adequate. For example, all staff should be reminded to report immediately to the safety officer any incident that might cause a risk to health or safety. The written statement could be included in each employee's contract of employment. The statement might be as follows:

Health and safety at work—The practice's policy on health and safety at work is to provide as safe and healthy working conditions as possible and to enlist the support of its employees towards achieving these ends. While the overall responsibility rests with your employer, all staff have legal duty to take reasonable care to avoid injury to themselves or to others by their work activities and not interfere with or misuse any clothing or equipment provided to protect health and safety. The main hazards that staff should be aware of are: (*i*) medical instruments, etc, in the consulting room; (*ii*) prams, bicycles, etc. Any accident to a member of the staff or a member of the public should be reported to the doctor in charge as soon as possible. You should record in writing a factual statement covering to the fullest possible extent all the circumstances of the accident at the time so that any necessary action may be taken to prevent a recurrence.

Maintaining the building

The general practitioner, "so far as is reasonably practicable as regards any place of work under (his) control," must ensure that the building is maintained in a safe condition, without risks to health. He must provide safe means of entrance and exit for his staff. But if the health centre is under the direct control of a health authority the general practitioner can only do what is reasonable on his part, and any blame may ultimately lie with the authority. For example, if there is loose guttering which the health authority is under a duty to maintain according to the licence between it and the practice, *so long as the general practitioner has notified the authority of the danger, preferably in writing*, he should be exonerated from liability if an accident does occur. He should, however, also follow up his letter to check that action was being taken by the authority. (Liability would fall on the authority under the Defective Premises Act 1972 and the Health and Safety at Work Act, since it is both the owner of the premises and those in control of maintenance who are responsible.) Similar considerations may arise when premises are rented from a private landlord. It may be advisable for a general practitioner to examine the licence or lease under which he holds the premises to clarify whose burden it is to maintain specific parts of the premises. The staff also have a responsibility to report any risks to health and safety.

A practice may not be exonerated of all responsibility for the safety of their premises, even if they are not the owners; they may be held responsible for hazards such as highly polished and slippery floors and unsafe electrical flex. But if the doctor is responsible for maintaining the premises he must concern himself with other parts, including, for example, the condition of steps and stairways, floors, and floor covering.

The Act also states that, as far as is reasonably practicable, the employer must provide and maintain a working environment for his employees that is without risk to health, with adequate provision for their general welfare. The wording appears to apply to more than just the physical environment of the employee. Here a practice would be well advised to consider whether there is an adequate rest room, refreshment facilities, and toilet and washing arrangements, etc. Again, the extent to which this can be done must depend on the practice's resources.

Safety representatives and safety officers

Not all practices will have safety representatives and safety committees. These are normally appointed only when trade unions are recognised for negotiating. In premises where there is more than one employer, however—for example, health centres—they will normally be required. Employee safety representatives can inspect the workplace, investigate accidents, make representations to the general practitioner, and also insist on a joint safety committee being appointed. Safety representatives have the legal right to challenge an employer on all matters affecting health and safety standards in the workplace.

But the Health and Safety Commission have recommended that similar arrangements for safety committees and safety representatives should be made even if staff are not unionised. The Health and Safety Commission think that since both the employer and employee share a statutory duty to ensure the health, safety, and welfare at work of all an employer may find it helpful if employees contribute to the development and improvement of health and safety procedures. The Commission have therefore recommended that in non-unionised workplaces the employer should set up a safety committee drawn from both management and staff. This is hardly practicable in a small practice, so the general practitioner may prefer to nominate a member of his staff to serve as the "safety officer" and monitor standards. The practice manager could well undertake this duty. The "safety officer" should report to the general practitioner who is the "controller" of the premises.

Duties to other users of premises

Although the purpose of the Health and Safety at Work Act is to ensure the safety of employees it also applies to all persons who enter the premises—ancillary staff employed by a health authority working on the premises, visitors, patients, and sundry "tradesmen" such as postmen, window cleaners, builders, and electricians. The Act imposes a duty on the general practitioner as the "controller" of the premises to ensure the safety of anyone who legitimately visits his premises. A health authority or a private landlord may also have a duty under the licence or lease, and they may also be liable if an accident occurs.

The law requires a general practitioner to conduct his practice in such a way so as to ensure, as far as is reasonably practicable, that all persons not in his employment who could be affected are not exposed to risks to their health and safety. This part of the Act links up with the civil liability of an occupier of premises under the Occupier's Liability Act 1957. It may be assumed that the standards expected under the Health and Safety at Work Act are equal to the "common duty of care" under the Occupier's Liability Act owed to all persons legitimately entering the premises. Under the civil law it is advisable for a general practitioner to anticipate who might be directly affected and to ensure that the premises are safe. The general practitioner would be well advised to consider whether there are any potential hazards for elderly or infirm patients.

The important difference between these duties and those to his own staff is that the staff should be provided with a written safety policy and be instructed and supervised on safety matters, and that quite specific arrangements should be made for their health, safety, and welfare. The Act is intended to protect people at work, but, almost as an afterthought, it has protected everybody who may be affected by the work.

Notifying accidents and dangerous occurrences

The regulations on notifying accidents and dangerous occurrences are relevant to general practitioners because they impose a statutory obligation on all employers to keep a record of accidents occurring on their premises and to notify the Health and Safety Executive of certain serious accidents. The general practitioner is liable as the "controller of the premises" to notify the Health and Safety Executive of certain accidents to his own staff and to anyone else who happens to be on the premises, such as patients, workmen, or health authority staff.

Accidents and dangerous occurrences may be divided into three categories:

(1) *Notifiable accidents*—These include fatal accidents (and those accidents that prove to be fatal within a year of their occurrence) and major injuries. A major injury is defined as a fracture of the skull, spine, pelvis, any bone in the leg (other than in the ankle or foot), any bone in the arm other than in the wrist or hand, amputation of a hand or foot, the loss of sight of any eye, or any other injury that results in the person injured being admitted into hospital as an inpatient for more than 24 hours, unless that person is detained only for observation.

These accidents must be reported to the Health and Safety Executive if they occur to anyone on the premises. There are two exceptions from the reporting requirements. In the unlikely event of injury occurring to a patient who is undergoing treatment in the surgery which is caused by the treatment it is not to be reported. Accidents to a self employed person working on the premises, unless he is under the control of another person, are also excluded from the reporting procedures.

(2) *Other accidents*—These do not have to be reported to the Health and Safety Executive. They include what are known in industry as "three day accidents." This category applies only to the general practitioner's own ancillary staff, not to other health authority employees working on his premises. These accidents are notified to the Health and Safety Executive by the Department of Health and Social Security (not by the general practitioner himself) only if the employee makes a claim for industrial injury benefit.

(3) *Dangerous occurrences*—These mostly apply to industrial premises; few are likely to happen in the general practitioner's premises. From the list of dangerous occurrences that have to be reported, only one type may be relevant. This is when a person is affected by the inhalation, ingestion, or other absorption of any substance, or lack of oxygen to an extent that it causes acute ill health requiring medical treatment. This could be caused by a defective central heating system.

HEALTH AND SAFETY AT WORK ACT 1974

Reporting accidents

The general practitioner would be responsible for reporting the accident, though in some circumstances responsibility would lie with the owner of the premises. It is advisable for the general practitioner to assume that he is responsible for notifying the Health and Safety Executive, even if he does not carry responsibility for the premises. Any notifiable accident must be directly notified to the local office of the Health and Safety Executive by telephone. It is advisable to keep a written record of the call, including the name of the civil servant receiving it, and the details of the accident as given over the telephone. Within seven days of the accident (or dangerous occurrence) taking place a written report on Form F2508 should be sent to the Health and Safety Executive by the doctor. If an accident in category (2) occurs, then the Department of Health will send an accident inquiry form to the general practitioner.

Written records

It is a legal requirement for every employer to keep an accident book on the premises. A record must be kept of all the notifiable accidents and dangerous occurrences, so that the employer can monitor these and identify any preventive action that should be taken. The Health and Safety Executive has published a record book, *Record of Accidents, Dangerous Occurrences and Ill-Health Enquiries* (F2509; £1·70; obtainable from HMSO). This accident book has space for 224 notifiable accidents and dangerous occurrences to be recorded, so it should last forever. A general practitioner, however, could adapt an exercise book for this purpose, and a copy of a page from the Health and Safety Executive accident book is shown for guidance (figure). Failure to apply these regulations could lead to a fine of up to £1000.

Oddly enough, at present the self employed person is exempt from the reporting procedure; a general practitioner need not report an accident to himself.

Building work on the premises

Serious hazards can arise when building work is in progress. The main contractor, subcontractor, and their employees have the prime duty to carry out their work in a safe manner. The general

Health and Safety Executive

Record of accidents and dangerous occurrences

Date of accident or dangerous occurrence	Place where accident or dangerous occurrence took place	Brief description of the circumstances	For accidents only				
1	2	3	Name of injured person 4	Sex 5	Age 6	Occupation 7	Nature of injury 8

practitioner's duty as the "controller" of the premises is to ensure that his staff, other employees on the premises, patients, and visitors are not put at risk. If unavoidable temporary hazards are caused by building operations these should be identified and their risks reduced as far as possible by providing warning notices that can be easily read by all persons using the premises. If a general practitioner is in any doubt about his responsibilities he may seek clarification from the local office of the Health and Safety Executive.

Clearing snow

A general practitioner may take steps to clear snow and ice from paths on the premises and from adjacent public pavements. Oddly enough, a good deed of this kind may well increase his liability to users of these pathways. If a person subsequently injures himself on a cleared pathway the person who has cleared the snow may be held liable. Uncleared snow carries no liability of this kind, since it is assumed that the person walking on it will exercise due care and attention.

Duties of the staff

Although the heaviest responsibilities lie with the general practitioner, reciprocal duties also lie with his staff. This is to ensure that the employer and his employees cooperate to provide a safe place of work. Employees should take reasonable care for their own health and safety and those of others who may be affected by their actions and omissions. They should cooperate with their employer or any other person—such as the health and safety inspector—who has responsibilities under the Act.

All employees have these duties to fulfil, both the general practitioner's own employees and any health authority staff. The duties on employees apply "while at work," throughout the time when they are in his employment "but not otherwise." What does "but not otherwise" mean? Would an employee be liable if an accident happened during a lunch or a tea break taken on the premises? It seems likely that any activities that are reasonably incidental to the employment—that is, the sort of activity a "reasonable" employee would indulge in—will be included—for example, making tea in the kitchen or using the toilet or washing facilities. This is important because messing facilities are often neglected but hazardous.

Every employee (and indeed any other person) is under a duty not to interfere with or misuse anything provided for the purpose of health and safety. This protects appliances and arrangements to ensure people's safety, such as fire escapes, fire extinguishers, and hazard warning notices. This could be extended to include interference with anything provided for welfare purposes, such as cloakroom and refreshment facilities. The extra responsibility placed upon employees by this Act is reflected in the far greater number of prosecutions against employees since it was implemented in 1975.

Enforcement

The Health and Safety at Work Act covers all "places of employment," and its inspectors therefore have the right to inspect general practitioners' premises. The Health and Safety Executive has divided Britain into areas, and each has its own team of inspectors. One group of inspectors is responsible for the "health services," which includes general practice premises.

Powers of the inspectors

Each inspector has a warrant of appointment that states his extensive powers, and the general practitioner may ask to see this for identification. An inspector normally has the right to enter any premises to enforce the Act. He does not have to seek the general practitioner's or any other person's permission, neither does he have to give notice of his visit. He may, however, only enter at a "reasonable time."

Inspectors normally give notice of their visits, and ring to make an appointment. Occasionally, however, some visits are "reactive" in response to a complaint from an employee or even a patient. Sometimes inspectors have made unannounced visits, not because they intend to cause offence or "catch" anybody off guard, but simply to slot the inspection of some small premises into a day's schedule of visits to larger premises. Although a surprise visit may be disconcerting, the general practitioner should not assume that the inspector has an ulterior motive. Oddly enough, it is because inspections of surgeries are still a comparatively rare event that some upset has been caused to the few general practitioners so far affected.

During his investigation the inspector can interview and take written statements from anyone who may have relevant information (and this could include patients as well as members of the ancillary staff). The inspector may want to obtain information to establish the facts about an accident or for evidence in legal proceedings. Any information provided will normally be treated as confidential. The information, however, may be subsequently disclosed if a prosecution is brought against the employer.

What will the inspector look for?

The inspector will wish to ensure that the general practitioner, if he employs five or more persons, has issued a statement of general policy on health and safety and any relevant instruction on safety procedures. He will expect an accident book to be kept on the premises. He will want to ensure that all electrical equipment is in safe working order and properly maintained. The normal standards applying to toilet and washing facilities in offices and shops should be met in the practice premises. He will undoubtedly expect to find a supply of hot and cold running water, and he may also recommend that wrist operated taps should be fitted in rooms used for examination and treatment of patients. Inspectors are also concerned about the condition of the heating plant, the arrangements for the storage of drugs, the condition of steam sterilisers, the standards of heating and lighting, and the procedure for the disposal of clinical waste. The *Statement of Fees and Allowances* provides for the direct reimbursement of any charges levied for the disposal of trade waste (see para 51.12(b)).

Improvement and prohibition notices

After completing his inspection the inspector will usually approach the person in administrative charge of the premises (often the practice manager) about any improvements to safety procedures and standards that may be required. If these are minor he will simply ask for them to be put right. If there is something more serious the inspector may write formally, or may serve a written notice requiring matters to be remedied. This is known as an Improvement Notice; it will specify a time limit of not less than 21 days within which the improvement must be made. The inspector must inform staff as well as the general practitioner of his intention to serve it. He may also bring a prosecution alleging a specific breach of a statutory provision.

If there is a serious risk to health and safety an inspector may issue a Prohibition Notice prohibiting the offending work activity. If the position is very grave the notice will take immediate effect, and work must stop at once; otherwise, a deferred Prohibition Notice may be issued stopping the work after a specified time.

The Improvement and Prohibition Notices are both served on the person carrying on or in control of the work in question, and this is normally done at the time of the inspection. The inspector should also advise of the procedure for appeal against the provisions of the notice. The general practitioner would usually receive the Notice, unless control of the practice had been delegated to a practice manager. When complied with, the Notices cease.

Offences and penalties

Because the Health and Safety at Work Act is a criminal statute contravention of its provisions may lead to a fine or imprisonment. Both the employer and his staff (as well as any other person on the premises) may be liable to prosecution. Furthermore, failure to carry out any duty under the Act is an offence and could also lead to prosecution. Verbal or written warnings, however, such as Improvement Notices, always precede any legal action. It is also an offence to obstruct an inspector in the performance of his duties and to contravene an Improvement or Prohibition Notice.

The Health and Safety Executive, as the enforcing authority, has the discretion to decide whether or not to prosecute and this decision is taken after advice from the inspector. Alongside a criminal prosecution of an employer, an employee could sue his employer for damages on the basis of employer's liability law, or simply for negligence. In any prosecution by the Executive account will be taken of what was reasonably practicable in the circumstances. This offers little consolation to a large employer but some comfort to the smaller employer with limited resources.

Crown premises—health centres

Although a health authority is a Crown body, it no longer enjoys certain exemptions from prosecution under the Act. Changes in health and safety legislation introduced in 1987 have removed

99

Crown immunity from NHS premises. But this does not reduce the liability of the general practitioner if he is the controller of the premises owned by the authority.

Fire precautions

Although the Fire Precautions Act 1971 is distinct from the Health and Safety at Work Act, general practitioners should be aware of its requirements. The general practitioner and his employees, together with any other people working on the premises, must for their own safety and for the safety of others see that there are adequate means of escape (unlocked, unobstructed, and usable when people are in the building) and also adequate fire fighting equipment that is properly maintained and readily available.

In large buildings where more than 20 people work, or where more than 10 people work other than on the ground floor the owner of the premises is required to obtain a certificate from the local fire authority regulating the means of escape and markings of fire exits. If the premises are owned by a health authority they are deemed to be Crown property, and the fire authority would be the Home Office, Scottish Home and Health Department, or Welsh Office. These premises should be equipped with properly maintained alarms and the employees should be familiar with the means of escape and the routine to be followed in the event of a fire, and they should have emergency lighting if this is necessary. Local fire inspectors ensure that premises comply with these statutory requirements. If you are in any doubt whether your premises require certification you should contact the fire prevention office of your local fire brigade.

Points to act on

(1) An accident book—for example, Health and Safety Executive Book, F2509 (which can be purchased from HMSO at £1·70), and copies of form 2508, the Accident Report Form—should be kept in an easily accessible place.

(2) You should prepare a written safety policy for all employees. Although this is mandatory only for those with five or more employees it is advisable for all general practitioners to prepare such a statement, even if it is brief and simple. This may be included in the employee's contract of employment.

(3) Regularly check any obviously hazardous areas—for example, unfinished building work, electrical equipment, loose floor covering—to see if there is anything that needs immediate attention.

(4) Ensure that electrical equipment is regularly maintained and serviced.

(5) Consider appointing a "safety officer"—this could be the practice administrator.

(6) Look at your lease or licence agreement to see who is responsible for the upkeep and repair of the premises. Consult your practice solicitor or the BMA if there is any doubt.

(7) Warning notices should inform patients and visitors of any hazards.

We are grateful to Dr John Ball, Dr Ewen Bramwell, Dr Arnold Elliott, and Dr Frank Wells for their advice. We are, of course, responsible for any omissions or errors.

Further reading

Free booklets available from the Health and Safety Executive

Health and Safety Commission. *Safety representatives and safety committees.* London: HMSO, 1977.

Health and Safety Commission. *The Act outlined.* London: HMSO, 1980.

Health and Safety Commission. *Advice to the self-employed.* London: HMSO, 1980.

Health and Safety Commission. *Advice to employers.* London: HMSO, 1975.

Health and Safety Commission. *Advice to employees.* London: HMSO, 1981.

Health and Safety Commission. *Some legal aspects and how they will affect you.* London: HMSO, 1975.

Health and Safety Commission. *Guidance notes on employer's statements for health and safety at work.* London: HMSO, 1980.

Health and Safety Executive. *Safety committees: guidance to employers whose employees are not members of recognised independent trade unions.* London: HMSO, 1979.

Health and Safety Executive. *Short guide to the Employer's Liability (Compulsory Insurance) Act 1969.* 1976.

Health and Safety Executive. *Reporting an accident.* 1980.

Free from the Home Office
Doctors and the Misuse of Drugs Act 1971. Home Office, 1978.
A guide to the Health and Safety at Work Act. London: HMSO. £2·75.
The notification of accidents and dangerous occurrences. London: HMSO. £2·75.
The safe disposal of clinical waste. London: HMSO. £1·50.

Statutory sick pay

The statutory sick pay scheme, which started on 6 April 1983, has greater administrative consequences for the employer than any other recent change in employment legislation. Indeed, its impact on the general practitioner's administrative procedures may be greater than any change since the introduction of PAYE (income tax) in 1948.

The Social Security and Housing Benefits Act 1982 introduces for the first time a statutory duty on employers to pay their staff during sickness absences on behalf of the state. Up to the introduction of the statutory sick pay scheme, sick pay as such had not been covered by legislation; the employer had discretion to decide whether or not to pay staff during absences for sickness. The only constraint on how this discretion was exercised had been any obligations arising from the contract of employment with his employees.

When writing about new legislation it is particularly rewarding to be able to suggest a course of action that can be easily understood and readily applied in general practice. A first impression of the new statutory sick pay scheme may be that it is complicated and difficult to administer. But if its principles are understood and a few simple preliminary and precautionary steps taken the general practitioner is unlikely to have serious difficulties. Advice and assistance may be obtained from the BMA regional staff and your local Department of Social Security office.

In common with other employment law the new sick pay legislation pays little regard to the limited resources of a small employer. Large organisations with personnel departments are anxiously trying to cope with this new legislation, and some are even using additional staff to implement it. The general practitioner has a far greater relative burden of additional administration, and this has to be borne by his existing practice staff. The revised DHSS booklet *Employer's Guide to Statutory Sick Pay*[1] is essential reading and may be obtained from your local DHSS office. This is an authoritative guide to the scheme and an essential reference document when you first have to pay sickness benefit. You should also obtain a supply of the three DSS forms for "transfer", "exclusion" and "leaving", which may have to be issued. Your sickness records should be reviewed, and if necessary amended, to ensure that they conform to the statutory requirements of the Act. Do no try to memorise the details of the scheme. It is through the practical experience of working out actual cases of the sickness scheme that you and your staff will become familiar with it. Administering the scheme should become a routine procedure, almost as familiar as PAYE (income tax).

If you are not an employer and your ancillary staff are employees of a local health authority you should take no action until you receive guidance from the employing authority.

It is reasonable to assume that most general practitioners do not have a formal sick pay scheme. Many doctors probably rely on a pragmatic approach when determining what pay their staff should receive during absence for sickness. They may even maintain their staff on full wages for short periods of absence, though this may mean that such staff, if they should claim state sickness benefit, would be financially better off during sickness than when working.

But when the period of sickness lengthens a general practitioner's decision to reduce or end sick pay may depend on various subjective considerations, including the value he attaches to the previous service of the sick employee, the length of previous service, and the likelihood of the employee returning to work within the foreseeable future. Only a few practices may have planned ahead for long term sickness, if only because this is regarded as a remote eventuality. Indeed, I would estimate that most general practitioners have not issued written contracts of employment to their staff, and this omission suggests that there is unlikely to be a formal sick pay scheme, although such a contract is not necessary to implement the new sick pay scheme.

Why has the statutory sick pay scheme been introduced?

Since 1948 the government has administered through the DSS a system of National Insurance sickness benefit. The Department has paid sickness and injury benefit claims made by employees within the National Insurance scheme. When an employee was sick his doctor was asked to complete a medical certificate on the prescribed form, which was submitted to the DSS to claim state benefits. These benefits were based on whether there were dependants and were tax free. The claim form was often submitted to the DSS by the employer because it was also used by the employer as evidence that the employee's absence from work was due to ill health. The form may also have been used to trigger payments under schemes for occupational sick pay. When this state scheme was introduced few employees were covered by occupational sick pay schemes; during the past 30 years, however, there has been a substantial growth in the coverage of these schemes. For many employees National Insurance sickness benefit is no longer an important element of their income during short term sickness.

The government has replaced this system by a statutory sick pay scheme for two main reasons. Firstly, it wishes to make sickness payments subject to taxation, thus preventing employees from "overbenefiting" when sick. Secondly, to eliminate the duplication of administration undertaken by civil servants and by employers. It intends to reduce the number of civil servants who administer the state sickness scheme by transferring to employers the responsibility for administering the basic state payments during sickness. In addition, the scheme is intended to increase the employer's awareness of his responsibility for monitoring and controlling the sickness absence of his employees. Self certification was a first important step in this direction.

Basic principles

The statutory sick pay scheme establishes a new minimum entitlement for sick pay for most employees. It replaces state sickness benefit for most periods of short term absence for sickness. The employer is required to pay sickness benefit as the agent of the government, but the decision on whether sick pay should be paid or not lies primarily with the employer, rather than with the DSS. This new statutory entitlement, however, does not prevent additional payments being made under an occupational sick pay scheme alongside the statutory sick pay scheme (or for those periods of sickness absence not covered by the statutory sick pay scheme). Indeed, a single payment may be made by the employer to cover both the new scheme and any occupational sick pay entitlements. The Act allows the employer to offset his liability to pay statutory sick pay against any contractual liability for sick pay.

How does "offsetting" work? If you are committed by contract to pay your employee for a day on which the employee was sick— for example, your practice's scheme for occupational sick pay or holiday pay—this payment will cover your liability for statutory sick pay so long as the amount you are paying is at least the appropriate level for that scheme. You do not have to pay statutory sick pay as well. More generally, if statutory sick pay is due to be paid on a certain day, any other payment that counts as earnings for the purposes of National Insurance contributions that you are already liable to make on that day will count towards your liability to pay statutory sick pay for that day.

The Social Security and Housing Benefits Act 1982 represents a radical new approach to sickness benefits, in that (*i*) all staff are covered by the Act and are entitled to statutory sick pay instead of state sickness or injury benefit for most periods of sickness unless for some reason they are excluded, and all employers are legally obliged to pay statutory sick pay; (*ii*) for those staff not covered by your own sick pay arrangements the new statutory scheme is usually their only source of income during sickness unless they qualify in addition for supplementary benefits; (*iii*) staff covered by your own occupational sick pay arrangements may continue to receive a higher level of sick pay than that due under the statutory scheme; (*iv*) both the statutory scheme and your own sick pay is paid by the practice; (*v*) long term sickness is still covered by the present National Insurance scheme, and staff will normally transfer from the statutory sick pay scheme to state invalidity benefit after 28 weeks' entitlement for statutory sick pay has been used up.

Summary

The main features of the scheme are:

(1) National Insurance sickness benefit is no longer payable for most sickness absence; instead your staff should receive sick pay directly from you.

(2) Sick pay is paid in the same way as normal pay and is liable to deductions for income tax and National Insurance contributions.

(3) Entitlement to sick pay does not depend on previous National Insurance contributions or previous service with the employer.

(4) Married women paying the reduced "stamp" and part timers are entitled to sick pay provided that their earnings are above £43.00 a week. (And part timers with more than one job may receive the full rates of sick pay simultaneously from several employers.) Sick pay is not paid for sickness during the first three unlinked waiting days, but for longer absences it will be paid for up to 28 weeks. The total sick pay that may be received from one employer for one or more periods of sickness, however, cannot exceed 28 weeks' worth. After 28 weeks of sick pay state benefit may be claimed from the DSS.

(5) If an employee changes jobs the new employer may also be liable to pay up to 28 weeks' sick pay, but should check whether payments have been made by the previous employer.

(6) You, as the employer, have to decide whether sick pay is payable.

(7) The employer can deduct the amount paid out in sick pay from subsequent remittances to the Inland Revenue for National Insurance contributions, and an extra amount to compensate for the employer's element of these.

How it works

Employers are responsible for payment of statutory sick pay to their employees for the first 28 weeks of sickness or injury at one of two flat rates. The appropriate flat rate will depend on the employee's average earnings. These rates of payment and the

earnings limits are reviewed annually by the Department of Social Security. The current rates effective from 6 April 1989 are:
—average weekly earnings of £84.00 or more: sick pay = £52.10 a week;
—average weekly earnings of £43.00—£83.99: sick pay = £36.25 a week.

These rates apply to all employees whether they are paying class 1 National Insurance contributions or the lower "stamp" under the current National Insurance benefit scheme. But there is no requirement to pay statutory sick pay if average earnings are below the National Insurance lower earnings limit, which is currently £43.00 a week. (To calculate average earnings, the general rule is to add together earnings over the 12 weeks up to and including the last pay day before the period of incapacity for work began and then to divide the total by 12. Any payment that is treated as earnings for the purpose of National Insurance contributions must be included and the gross figure (before National Insurance or other deductions are made) must be used.)

The employer will be able to recover from the DSS the amount of sick pay that he has paid out by deducting them from his monthly National Insurance contributions and PAYE (income tax) to the Inland Revenue. At the end of the 28 week statutory sick pay the DSS will normally accept responsibility for payment of sickness or injury benefit, except for employees who pay the married women's reduced National Insurance rate. This will be as at present dependant related and tax free. (The government also intends to bring these benefits into taxable income.)

The Act allows the employer to offset his liability for the statutory sick pay scheme against any contractual liability for sick pay. Thus, for example, if a general practitioner is already committed to paying £52.10 a week or more sick pay according to his existing sick pay arrangements and he is obliged to pay £52.10 a week statutory sick pay he would be able to continue to pay his own rate of sick pay and to recover £52.10 per week from his National Insurance contributions.

The detailed rules for determining when payments for sickness absence should be made are clearly set out in the DSS's

Employer's Guide to Statutory Sick Pay.[1] The check list below will help general practitioners to decide when payments should be made. An employee's entitlement to sick pay depends on three main conditions:

(*i*) that the day of absence forms part of a *period of incapacity for work*—any four or more consecutive calendar days when the employee is incapable of doing work of a type that he or she might reasonably be expected to do under the contract of employment due to specific disease or bodily or mental disablement constitute a period of incapacity for work;

(*ii*) that the day of absence is part of a *period of entitlement*—that is, during which the employee would be expected to carry out the continuing contract of employment, not having exhausted her entitlement to sick pay or being excluded for certain other reasons from entitlement to it; a period of entitlement will occur in most cases;

(*iii*) that the day is a *qualifying day*—that is, a day or days on which the employee would normally be required by the general practitioner to be available for work by her contract or which is agreed between the general practitioner and his employee to reflect the terms of that contract. In most circumstances qualifying days will be those days normally worked.

Statutory sick pay, together with any payments made under occupational sick pay schemes (except for those schemes based on trusts and insurance companies), is subject to PAYE (income tax) and to employer's and employee's National Insurance contributions just like normal pay. It is also permissible to make other deductions from statutory sick pay, such as the employee's contributions to occupational pension scheme, savings arrangements, or any other deductions that are made under normal circumstances from an employee's pay.

Who is eligible to receive statutory sick pay?

In general all employees are covered by the new sick pay scheme if they are sick four or more consecutive days. But there are circumstances when there is no liability to pay (table I). If your employee is off sick and is in one of these groups you must tell her why you are not paying for sickness absence so that she can claim state sickness benefit instead. The law requires you to complete an "exclusion form" (SSP1(E)) and give or send it to the employee (together with any sick notes) not later than seven days after you have been notified of her sickness. This exclusion form tells the employee and the DSS why you are not paying for sickness absence and provides the employee with a claim form for state sickness benefit. Your local DSS office will supply copies of the form. You are of course free to pay your own sick pay to any employee who is not eligible to receive statutory sick pay.

TABLE I—*Who does not receive statutory sick pay?*

You do not have to pay an employee who is over minimum state pension age at the time of going sick;

Or was taken on for a short term contract of fewer than three months;

Or has average weekly earnings less than the lower limit for National Insurance contribution liability;

Or goes sick within 57 days of a previous claim for one of these state benefits: sickness benefit, invalidity pension, maternity allowance, and unemployment benefit, but in only very limited circumstances;

Or has done no work for you under the contract of service;

Or is off sick during the time starting 11 weeks before her expected week of confinement and ending six weeks after;

Or has already been due 28 weeks' statutory sick pay from you and has not requalified;

Or is sick while abroad outside the European Community;

Or is in legal custody;

Or goes sick during a stoppage of work, unless she has not taken part in the dispute and has no direct interests in it

(The "exclusion form" SSP(E) lists these groups of employees)

Deciding when to pay

You may first know about the employee's sick absence when she does not come to work. You will expect her to report the absence (table II) and if, according to the regulations for statutory sick pay, her notification is late you may opt to withhold sick pay (table III). But you should be very cautious about withholding sick pay, and no action should be taken before seeking advice from your local DSS office. If sick pay is withheld you will need to formally notify your employee. She may then appeal against your decision through the DSS local office. You may not need to change your present rules for reporting sickness absence. But if these are more stringent than the statutory sick pay regulations require, an employee who is regarded as late in notifying sickness for your purposes may not be late for the sick pay scheme. You are entitled to ask for reasonable evidence of incapacity. The type of evidence

109

required for statutory sick pay and when it may be requested are summarised in table IV.

For the purposes of determining when sick pay is payable, a day of sickness is a day on which the employee is incapable, because of a specific illness or disablement, of doing work that she can reasonably be expected to do under her contract of employment. Only complete days of sickness count for the scheme.

TABLE II—*Notification of sickness absence*

Employers usually have rules about the time by which an employee should notify sickness. Your current arrangements may be appropriate for the purpose of the statutory sick pay scheme. The regulations provide that:

(*i*) you must make it clear to your employees how you want to be notified of sickness—for example, by telephone, in writing, or both

(*ii*) you may not require notification earlier than the first qualifying day in a period of sickness

(*iii*) you may not require notification by a specific time of day

(*iv*) notification in writing must be regarded as having been made on the day of posting

(*v*) notification may be made by proxy

(*vi*) you may not *require* notification in the form of medical evidence

(*vii*) you may not require notification more often than once a week during sickness

You do not need to change your practice rules, but if these are more strict you may find that a notification that is regarded as "late" by your rules is nevertheless acceptable for the statutory sick pay scheme

TABLE III—*Late notification of sickness absence*

If an employee is late in notifying sickness without reasonable cause you may withhold sick pay

But you may only withhold sick pay if there was no good cause for the delay in notification

There is an absolute time of 91 days for notifying a day of incapacity, after which payment cannot be made even if there was a good reason for the delay

Each employer has to apply common sense and judgment in deciding if there was good cause for late notification

TABLE IV—*Evidence of sickness*

You are entitled to ask for reasonable evidence of incapacity—for example, a self certificate for periods of up to seven days or a doctor's statement for periods after the first seven days

You may use your own self certification forms

Your responsibility is to satisfy yourself that your employee is incapable of working under her contract; whether you accept the evidence presented is for you to decide

It is interesting that a certificate of incapacity for work may be received from someone who is not a registered medical practitioner, including osteopaths, chiropractors, Christian Scientists, herbalists, and acupuncturists, but "a doctor's statement is strong evidence of incapacity and should usually be accepted as conclusive evidence" (*Employer's Guide to Statutory Sick Pay*[1])

Before sick pay is owing there must be four or more consecutive days of sickness. Sundays and public holidays are included in this calculation. (Thus if an employee has a short spell of sickness just before or after a weekend you will need to know whether she was incapable of work on Saturday and Sunday.) This is called a "period of incapacity for work." If there are fewer than four consecutive days of sickness there is no "period of incapacity for work" and no action should be taken under the scheme.

Sick pay is not necessarily paid for all days in a period of incapacity for work since it has to be paid only for "qualifying days" of sickness (table V). Moreover, it is not payable for the first three qualifying days in any period of incapacity since these are the waiting days. For example, your receptionist, who has five agreed qualifying days a week—Monday to Friday inclusive—is sick for one week starting on Monday. If she is eligible for sick pay Monday, Tuesday, and Wednesday will be waiting days and sick pay will be due on Thursday and Friday.

TABLE V—*Qualifying days*

Qualifying days are the only days for which sick pay is payable, and are the only days that count as waiting days. They are: the days agreed between you and your employee—these will normally be the days of the week on which an employee is required by his contract to be available for work, or days chosen to reflect the pattern of working. For example, if your receptionist works on a rota system you may agree qualifying days that follow the pattern of working exactly, or you may agree that the same days of each week will be qualifying days

You are free to choose which days you wish, as long as you and your employee are in agreement. But there is an overriding rule. Any agreement must provide at least one qualifying day in each week

If you cannot reach agreement the qualifying days will be those days on which the employee would actually have worked if she had not been sick—but the overriding rule still holds. If your receptionist would not have worked in a particular week the regulations provide that Wednesday of that week will be regarded as a qualifying day

In the absence of a clear indication of which days would have been working days in any week the regulations provide that every day of that week, except standard rest days, will be qualifying days

These rules allow for great flexibility in the way that qualifying days may be agreed with your employees. If you are already committed to paying your own occupational sick pay you should aim at maximising receipt of sick pay to offset this

Periods of incapacity for work that are separated by eight weeks—that is, 56 calendar days—or less are said to be linked: they count together as a single period. Thus if two or more periods are linked then there can be no more than three waiting days in all.

Your maximum liability to pay statutory sick pay is defined as follows. The maximum amount payable is 28 weeks, and liability continues as long as the period of incapacity for work (or linked periods of incapacity) lasts subject to the 28 weeks limit. Separate periods of incapacity are linked as long as they are not separated by more than eight weeks. There is a three year limit to any linking of periods of incapacity. If your employee's sickness continues after your liability for sick pay ends she may be able to claim state sickness benefit. To make this transfer to the state scheme as smooth as possible, you must give a sick employee a DHSS "transfer form" SSP1(T).

How should it be paid?

Because statutory sick pay can be paid only for qualifying days the daily rate is the appropriate weekly rate divided by the number of qualifying days in the week (beginning with Sunday). For example, for an employee who works five days a week the agreed qualifying days are Monday to Friday inclusive. If she qualifies for the standard rate of sick pay—£52.10 a week—her daily rate will be £10.42. Sick pay is normally paid when you would have paid your employee wages for the same period. In most cases you will pay it on the same day that you pay occupational sick pay. The legislation provides for sick pay to be offset against any payment that you may make from your own scheme for occupational sick pay.

How to recover the money you have paid out

You may deduct the gross amount of sick pay that you have paid from the total amount of employers' (primary) and employers' (secondary) class 1 National Insurance contributions owing to the collector of taxes for the tax month in which the sick pay was paid (or for contributions owing for subsequent months). If the amount of sick pay that you are entitled to recover exceeds the total of your National Insurance contributions and PAYE income tax due that month you should, if possible, carry forward the excess and then deduct it from payments due to the collector of taxes for the following month(s). But if you want to recover the excess quickly you may write to the collector for payment. Errors are likely to occur when employers and their staff are unfamiliar with the scheme. Any error, whether it is an inaccuracy in your records or a wrong payment, should be reported immediately to your local DSS office, and you should await advice on how to proceed.

When you should stop paying

You should not pay sick pay to an employee for any period after: (*i*) she is no longer incapable of work—for example, if she returns to work or stops sending doctor's statements; (*ii*) she has been due

28 weeks' sick pay at the appropriate weekly rate; (*iii*) she reaches the 11th week before the week in which her baby is due; (*iv*) her contract of services comes to an end; (*v*) she goes abroad outside the European Community or is taken into legal custody.

Points to act on

There are several steps you should have taken to prepare yourself for its introduction:

(1) Agreed with your staff which days will serve as qualifying days. These will usually be those days normally worked, including Saturdays if applicable.

(2) Decided on a system of notification of illness and told your staff what this is. Your staff must know when you require notification and what evidence of incapacity is required.

(3) Obtained a supply of the relevant DSS forms. SSP1(T) for the transfer of staff to the National Insurance state benefit scheme, SSP1(E) to exclude staff from payment of sick pay, and SSP1(L) for some leavers.

(4) Made sure your record keeping complies with what is required under the new law. Form SSP2 could serve as a record sheet and is available free from the DSS.

(5) Obtained your free copy of the DHSS's revised *Employer's Guide to Statutory Sick Pay.*[1] This 43 page booklet provides the most authoritative statement of the scheme.

(6) If you have further doubts or worries the staff of the BMA regional offices are available to advise and help BMA members.

(7) If you are already committed to paying your own occupational sick pay your objective should be to arrange with your staff the qualifying days so that you may obtain the maximum reimbursement of statutory sick pay as a contribution towards offsetting your own sick pay.

Keeping records

You are required by law to keep the following sickness absence records: (*i*) dates of sickness absence of at least four consecutive days (including Saturdays and Sundays) reported to you by your employees; (*ii*) any days within these sickness absences for which statutory sick pay was *not* paid, together with the reasons for not paying; (*iii*) details of each employee's qualifying days in each period of incapacity.

All these records should be kept in a form that allows an inspector from the Department of Social Security to have access to them on request, and you must be able to produce them within a reasonable time if you are asked to do so. They are, of course, your source of information if an employee asks you for a written statement of his or her entitlement to statotury sick pay for a past period.

As long as the records conform to these requirements they may be kept in any way that is convenient to you. You must retain them for at least three years after the end of the tax year to which they relate. There is a penalty for failure to comply (see table). The DSS has produced a record sheet (form SSP2), which has been designed solely for this scheme. Sheets are available free from local DSS offices.

You are also required by law to keep records showing, for each pay day and for each employee, sick pay that is paid as well as the usual records of pay, PAYE income tax, and National Insurance contributions. And when making your annual returns of pay, tax, and National Insurance contributions to the collector of taxes, you must also provide details of the gross amount of sick pay paid to each employee and the total amount paid to all employees during the tax year. Full details of what is required are given in the *Employer's Guide to PAYE* (booklet P7) (available from any tax office), leaflet NP15 (paragraph 114–119) (available from any DSS office), and the *Employer's Guide to Statutory Sick Pay* (paragraphs 182–192).[1]

In addition to the above records that you are legally obliged to keep there are other records that you may find useful to keep for your own purposes. (1) Any doctor's statements or sick notes; you may wish to retain or copy the originals, since if there should be some dispute about days of sickness knowledge of the date on which the doctor signed the sick note, when you received it, the period it covered, and the nature of the illness could be useful. (2) Details of your rules on the notification of sickness, and the dates on which your employees notified you of sickness. This information will be useful if there is any dispute about eligibility for statutory sick pay.

How sick pay affects the direct reimbursement of staff salaries

Unless some adjustment is made to the directly reimbursed

114

Offences and penalties

The Social Security and Housing Benefits Act 1982 and its regulations provide

Offence	Penalty
(1) Failure to pay sick pay within the time allowed, when an insurance officer, local tribunal, or commissioner has given a formal decision that it is payable	(1) (*a*) For any one offence, a fine not exceeding £400 (*b*) For continued failure to pay sick pay after conviction, a further fine of up to £20 for each day of such failure
(2) Failure to keep the required records in connection with sick pay	(2) (*a*) For any one offence, a fine not exceeding £400 (*b*) For continued failure to keep such records after conviction, a further fine of up to £20 for each day of such failure
(3) Failure by an employer to provide an employee with the prescribed information, by the prescribed time, in connection with a claim for: sickness benefit, maternity allowance, invalidity pension, industrial injuries benefit, non-contributory invalidity benefit— that is, failure to provide an exclusion or transfer form	(3) (*a*) For any one offence, a fine not exceeding £400 (*b*) For continued failure to provide such information after conviction, a further fine of up to £20 for each day of such failure
(4) Producing, furnishing, or causing or knowingly allowing to be produced or furnished, any document or information that is known to be false in a material particular when purporting to recover amounts paid by way of statutory sick pay	(4) A fine not exceeding £2000 or a term of imprisonment not exceeding three months, or both
(5) Recklessly producing or furnishing any document or information that is false in a material particular, when purporting to recover amounts paid by way of statutory sick pay	(5) A fine not exceeding £1000
(6) Failing to provide, when requested in writing to do so information required by an insurance officer, a local tribunal, a social security commissioner, or the Secretary of State for Social Services of his authorised representatives, for the formal determination of any question arising in connection with statutory sick pay	(6) (*a*) For any one offence, a fine not exceeding £400 (*b*) For continued failure to provide such information after conviction, a further fine of up to £20 for each day of such failure
(7) Failure to provide information about entitlement, e.g. a "leaver's" statement	(7) A fine not exceeding £400

salaries of trainees and ancillary staff who continue to be paid when sick there will be an element of double payment to doctors. It has been agreed that: (*a*) trainers should inform family practitioner committees of the amount of statutory sick pay paid and recovered

STATUTORY SICK PAY

Procedure for statutory sick pay

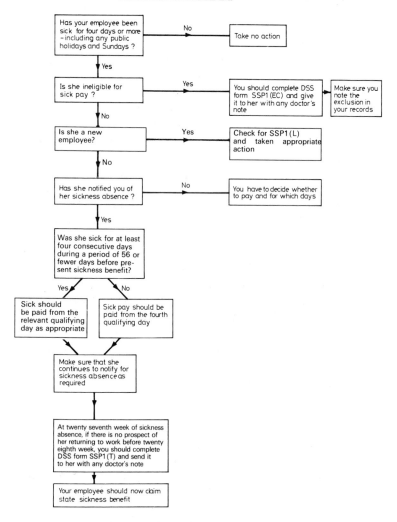

when their trainees are sick and that family practitioner committees should reimburse the trainees' salaries net of sick pay; (b) doctors should, when informing family practitioner committees of the salaries paid to staff under the ancillary staff scheme, declare the amount of sick pay paid and recovered when their staff are sick and this will be set against the amount directly reimbursed by family practitioner committees. The *Statement of Fees and Allowances* (the "Red Book") has been amended accordingly.

Examples of how statutory sick pay works

(1) Your receptionist works six days each week, Monday to Saturday, and you have agreed that her qualifying days should be Monday to Saturday inclusive. Although she only works half days on Wednesdays and Saturdays, all six working days count as qualifying days. Your rules about notifying sickness absences are that employees must telephone on the first qualifying day of sickness.

Your receptionist does not come to work on Monday, 14 November, and she telephones you that morning to say that she is ill. She returns to work on Tuesday, 22 November, and completes a sick certification form, saying that she was sick from Sunday, 13 November until Tuesday, 15 November, and provides a doctor's statement dated 16 November, which states that she will be fit to return to work on 22 November. Her weekly earnings are £125 gross. Her appropriate weekly rate of statutory sick pay is £52.10 and her daily rate is £52.10 ÷ 6 = £8.68 (the weekly rate divided by the number of qualifying days in the week).

The first three qualifying days, 14 15 and 16 November are waiting days for which sick pay is not payable. Sick pay would be payable for 17, 18, 19, and 21 November at £8.68 per day, making a total of £34.72. But since you are already paying her full pay of £125 per week (£20·83 for each day of sickness absence), which is well in excess of your liability for sick pay for each payable day, you need pay no more than this. Your liability for sick pay has been more than met by your own sick payments, but you should, of course, reclaim the gross amount of sick pay due (£34.72) by deducting this from your next monthly payment of National Insurance contributions and PAYE (income tax).

(2) Your practice nurse works on mornings only—each Wednesday, Thursday, and Friday. You have not agreed any qualifying days with her in advance (although you should have done), but she is aware of your rule about notification of sickness, which says that employees should telephone you on the first day of absence.

She does not come in to work on Wednesday, 1 June, but telephones that day to say that she is ill. It is her first absence for over a year. As a part timer she is not entitled to any occupational sick pay from you.

On Monday, 6 June you receive a self certificate form stating that she has been incapable of work since Saturday, 28 May, together with a doctor's statement dated 4 June, which states she will be fit to return to work on Friday, 10 June. She returns to work on that day.

Her pay over the eight weeks before she fell sick has been £45 a week gross, payable each Friday. Which days are qualifying days? In the absence of any agreement as to qualifying days, they are those days that you and your employee agree would normally have been worked—that is, Wednesday, Thursday, and Friday. Thus there are three qualifying days in each week.

The weekly rate of statutory sick pay is £36.25, being the lower of the two flat rates. The appropriate daily rate is therefore £36.25 ÷ 3 = £12.08.

This spell of sickness included five qualifying days. The first three are waiting days, and sick pay is therefore only payable on 8 and 9 June. Since the daily rate is £12.08, the total gross sick pay due is £24.16. This should be reclaimed in the normal way by deducting it from your monthly payment of National Insurance contributions and PAYE (income tax).

(3) Two of your receptionists have a job sharing arrangement; they fill one post by working alternate weeks. One of these receptionists is sick on Monday, 11 July, a day in the week when she would not normally be working. On Wednesday, 13 July you receive a doctor's statement stating that she will be fit to return to work on Thursday, 21 July. Your receptionist is paid £260 gross each calendar month. Her average weekly pay will be (£260 × 12) ÷ 52 = £60.

You have agreed that her qualifying days should be those days on which she would normally work—Monday to Friday—and you have regarded each week as a normal working week even though she works alternate weeks, simply because the two receptionists sometimes vary by agreement the sequence of their rota. (You are free to agree any pattern of qualifying days so long as there is at least one qualifying day in each week. Indeed, if you had limited the qualifying days to Monday to Friday on alternate weeks, the

Wednesday in the week not normally worked would have been deemed a qualifying day.)

The number of qualifying days on which statutory sick pay is due is five: 11, 12, and 13 July are waiting days. The weekly rate of sick pay is £36.25—the lower level of payment. The daily rate of sick pay is £36.25 ÷ 5 = £7.25. Total gross sick pay due is £7.25 × 5 = £36.25. You already pay half pay for sickness, and your receptionist will have been paid 5/22nd × £130 = £29.55 for her five qualifying days on which sick pay is payable. She is therefore due to receive a further £6.70 to comply with the scheme.

(This is calculated by dividing the total number of working days in July—22—by the number of qualifying days on which statutory sick pay was payable and you also paid your own sick pay.)

I thank Dr John Ball and the late Dr W G A Riddle for advice. Any omissions or errors are mine.

Reference

[1] Department of Health and Social Security. *Employer's Guide to Statutory Sick Pay*. London: DHSS, October 1985.

Index